Instinctive Swimming

A new way of learning to swim

Translation: KMK Biuro Tlumaczen Elzbieta Plaskowska
Methodical Consultation: Dawid Tatarczyk
Proofreading: Karolina Kadluczka
Cover graphic: Malgorzata Margo Chaja
Cover and graphic design: Bogumila Celuch
Text Compostion: InkWander
Technical correction: Karolina Kadluczka
Video composition: Maciej Leon Myszka
Training consultation: Marcin Chojnacki

ISBN: 9788397177949

Limitless Mind Publishing Ltd
15 Carleton Road
Chichester
PO19 3NX
England
Tel. +44 7747761146
Email: office@limitlessmindpublishing.com

Dear Reader!

Find us on Facebook/Instagram:
limitless mind publishing
And visit our page on Amazon
by entering: limitless mind publishing into the search bar
or by scanning the QR code to see our other titles.

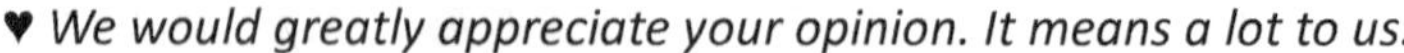

♥ *We would greatly appreciate your opinion. It means a lot to us.*

I would like to thank my wife Monika and our daughters Hania and Lilka for their understanding and dedication.

Thank you for allowing me to pursue my passion for swimming, none of it is possible without you.

Contents

A different kind of foreword

I've never liked books about swimming. I was discouraged and quickly bored with the theoretical, scientific language and the pretentious narrative. I was somehow unable to find a link between these worlds: the wonderful harmony and coordination of the human body with which you could almost literary fly in water, and the mechanical and scientific descriptions of drills, tables, human physiology, and sports training.

Working in various swimming pools for the last fifteen years, I have carefully observed the course and methodology of swimming lessons and training in different strokes. I got the same impression – it was all so unremarkable: kickboard, repeating arm movements, leg action, waiting for the child to "get hold of it".

From the beginning, I had a completely different approach to swimming. I believed it was first and foremost a form of art, while mechanics and physiology come as second and third. To be honest, I was initially a bit ashamed of my idea, being aware of the depths of my ignorance about the intricacies of so-called "sports" swimming. I felt that being sensitive to the beauty of this sport, I have no right to barge into this scientific and mechanical world of hard and monotonous drills to find a place for myself.

Over time, when I was still expanding my knowledge, at times I felt I have already mastered the technique, mechanics, and human physiology, only to doubt myself again, and this regular patter of ups and downs will probably continue to mark my adventure with swimming. However, the perceived essence of the art of swimming, of the great, eternally unfathomable secret of its beauty, remained inside me; in fact, it has become the only true meaning.

Despite the ups and downs of my career as a swimming coach, my experience with working with both small children who are afraid of water, and Olympians striving to improve their results by a few tenths of a second, at various school, club, national and international swimming competitions, I still feel that by helping someone fly in the water, I contribute to creating beauty.

This book is a reminiscence of the many years of observation, professional experience, countless hours of classes with children, training sessions, conversations, disputes, experiments, but most of all – continuous learning, both from the great masters of swimming, as well as early-stage enthusiasts who only start their career in this profession. I have been learning from outstanding athletes competing at the Olympic Games and from six-year-olds who were figuring out how to freely float on the water and move forward.

In this book, I present a new way of working with young swimmers. I hope to make your work as a teacher, instructor, or swimming coach exceptionally effective, but above all – extremely passionate.

About the method

The instinctive swimming method is based on two training premises.

First, it is a fusion of knowledge obtained from swimming coaches, educators, and child psychologists. It is also based on the present-day knowledge of the swimming technique, the evolution of training, and my own experience.

The second premise of the instinctive swimming method is the form of communication in which the nuances of the swimming technique are personified and animated. This helps the children soak up the skills and knowledge in a play-based training strategy. Meeting the contemporary needs and sensation capabilities of children belonging to the generation brought up by "talking heads" from smartphone screens is no easy task, but the greatest potential for acquiring knowledge and skills still lies in the children's imagination.

When this method is used with children who cannot swim, they relatively quickly gain the freedom to safely and independently move in deep water, learn to feel the water on their hands and feet, and they soon acquire a sense of balance in the water.

The four styles trained according to the instinctive swimming method are characterized by an optimal index of movement frequency in relation to the stroke length, highly effective leg action, and the unique swimming aesthetics originating from the water sensation. The technique of each swimming style can be modified and expanded, adapted to the distance or the trainer's concept.

The most essential training content from the book is illustrated in specially created videos, accessible via QR code.

Enough of these stories, let's get to the bottom of it. We set out to the sea fully prepared for some adventure in the unfamiliar waters of the instinctive swimming method.

Prologue

The weather was warm. February of that year was the quintessence of winter, but it seemed to give way for some warmer tones that early afternoon. The sun was shining through the pale grey clouds, and the wind stopped completely. I felt upbeat, despite the overwhelming four months of gray-dark cold in which my countrymen spend almost half of their life. I was waiting for the arrival of an exceptional swim coach who for many years had argued that technique is the foundation of children's training and the basis of all swimming in general. I have heard stories about him, I was a little afraid of him, but I also admired him a lot. The smoke of yet another cigarette thickened in the air, a circle chasing a circle. At one point a silver PT Cruiser slowly drove into the parking lot of the sports center where I had been staying for several days with my athletes attending a training camp. The man I had been waiting for got out of this little car, which resembled a London taxi. He was wearing a black, floor-length sheepskin coat with beautiful ornaments and an enormous collar. "What a bird of paradise!" – a thought crossed my head. He came straight from Vienna to tell me about his concept of swimming lessons and to explore the options of a joint venture of some kind. A few hours later, in a tiny hotel room, I was listening to him and looking at him to finally begin to understand. We talked about jazz, a Miles Davis concert, how a trumpet can play an incredibly quiet piano... But most of all, we discussed about the essence of swimming, flying in water thanks to... water. The most basic human ability, not driven by any force or a trained trajectory of movement.

We met again in late spring. We spent ten days together, the trainer demonstrated how he developed the swimming skills in children. We held a swimming training of several days, where I could see with my own eyes how his training concepts worked in the children who wanted to learn to swim. The coach has held such a workshop many times before, but I was completely new to it.

These two meetings redirected my thoughts and actions concerning the swimming technique to new and unexpected dynamics. They helped me gain the knowledge about swimming skills that I present in the first part of this book, and allowed me to develop the training method that I have called "instinctive". The knowledge and ideas of Andrzej Szarzyński is what inspired me most to write this book.

Discovering the innate swimming skills

Can humans swim?

It is not clear whether the ability to swim is encoded in the human genotype, just as the skills of walking, running, jumping or throwing. But one thing is certain: when thrown into the water, mammals (except for apes) do swim, without any previous drills with a kickboard or being explained how to move arms or legs.

Does this also apply to humans? You may think all humans can swim instinctively when watching YouTube videos of how babies turn over on their backs and float freely on the water surface when thrown into a swimming pool, they indeed do it instinctively. However, this skill must be first unlocked by an experienced infant swimming instructor who works with these babies. Therefore, even in this most instinctive period of ontogenesis, it takes someone with the proper knowledge and skills to get this ability unleashed in water.

I will say it loud and clear – the hypothesis about the natural swimming ability of human beings is absolutely true, but only after the right conditions are created. All the training work to be done with and by people who are theoretically unable to swim must be meticulously carried out so that this extremely delicate process develops smoothly and harmoniously. Bean seeds placed on a jar of water and gauze to germinate need water and light instead of high-quality fertilizers and growth accelerators.

This is where we introduce the new figure of a swimming instructor. He is not a teacher, but a guide who guides a person – using the appropriate methods – to discover and develop the natural swimming skills.

The chapter on basic swimming is built around this concept: we do not teach, but guide the trainees to develop the skills they inherited from their ancestors.

Activating swimming skills in humans

Stress is main reason why a person is unable to float and comfortably move in water when thrown into deep water. This psychological state of mental and physical imbalance precludes any chance of activating the two premises of swimming – the sensation of water and a body position that provides enough buoyancy.

When thrown into deep water, a stressed non-swimmer will first try to stand on legs, which is a natural position for a two-legged human being, and will then desperately look for a grip, something solid to hold on to.

A standing position in water with the head in one line with the spine is the least stable one, and provides the lowest possible buoyancy control. The psycho-physical imbalance is getting deeper and deeper when the person feels a precipice rather than a solid foundation under the feet.

The palms of the hands appear to be the last resort as they harbor the highest number of proprioceptors respond to stimuli such as touch. However, stress reduces the sensation on the palms, and they certainly cannot feel the water pressure, which is the only form of grip in the water.

What's left to do? A drowning person thrusts their arms up in a last-ditch effort to get some help. And then the head will definitely sink into the water because of the raised up arms and the vertical body position in the water.

Therefore, our first task as a guide in the world of swimming will be to create conditions for children to contain stress, especially during the initial classes.

What should you do first? Just have a little chat. Ask the children their names, how old they are, what vegetables they don't like, which flavor is the best. As a matter of fact, all this must take place at some distance from the pool.

If children are left alone in a new unfamiliar world, an adult acting as their guardian has immense authority and respect among them. They will believe virtually everything you tell them about water and swimming. This "handicap" is your greatest asset.

A tale of magic water that can lift a human

This seemingly trivial story is the first, most important step on the path to unlock the instinctive swimming skills. First and foremost, it reduces the feeling of stress as it stimulates the imagination, and helps build an inner conviction that this story is in fact true.

How do you tell the story to the children? In whatever way you want. But just tell them that water is truly magical and that people can be floating on it.

"Okay, okay, it's just a tale, it's not true," the children may replay.

"Yeah? See for yourself."

Move closer to the pool, seat the children so that they feel safe, and immerse yourself in the water on the deepest lane. The children will watch you do that: you will be lying on your back in the water, with no fins or any other gear while talking to them. Ooh, it might actually be true – they might think – Well, he is my trainer, he is definitely a great swimmer and that's why he floats on water. Now take the next step forward to prove that water is magical. Ask one of the children to sit close to the water so that they can touch you. Then tell everyone:

"Look, he/she will now push me under the water and I will swim to the surface without moving my legs and arms."

Inhale while standing vertically in the water, and let the kid push you under the water. The air in the lungs will bring you to the surface. Everyone is watching you.

"Ooh, the water itself lifts the coach up... It really is magical!"

After that ask each of the children to push you under the water. We've nailed it!

Now the children have to find out for themselves. This is where the next stage of training begins as you have to create conditions in deep water so that children can float safely. They trust you, after all, they saw you being raised by the water up to the surface. Standard swimming sleeves are the best swimming gear at this stage. They provide the most reliable standing position when you put them on the shoulders, and they raise the body high enough so that the whole head and neck are above the water. When wearing sleeves, children do not desperately search for a solid surface under their feet, but are able to float comfortably, which creates ideal conditions for developing the water sensation on their feet.

Children descend down the pool ladder into the water one by one, and you keep an eye on them while in the water.

"How do you feel? Do you feel that the water is holding you?"

"It really holds me, you were right!"

Of course, some children will be less confident, some of them will stick to the edge of the pool, reluctant to start flying in the magical water for the first time. Why is this happening? Because they are simply too scared, for various reasons that are very difficult to pin down. And now what? Just leave them alone. Some people need more time to integrate with the new environment, and they cannot be forced to do anything. One thing is certain: they will ultimately join the rest of the group in the fun activities, taking one small step at a time. The natural desire to join other members of the group is your best tool as a coach.

Activating the water sensation on the feet

When most of our children stand freely in the water, or even move around in deep water wearing the sleeves, take the children out of water to the side of the pool. Now focus on the foot's dorsum where you wear your shoelaces. These will be the wind feathers with which the children will soon start to fly better in the water. Ask the children to pat their hands on the dorsum of their feet, and then to tap a rubber ball with their foot several times, so that the entire surface of the instep of the foot is in contact with the ball. Then go into the water again. Once everyone is in the water (with the sleeves on), ask the children to imagine the ball is under the water and try to kick it in the same way with the left and the right leg several times.

The Water-Kissel, part 1

Let's return to the place where the children used to pat their feet. Now ask them to kick the water ball again, but now focus on something else: if the water starts to get thick like a kissel[1], it means that a wing feather has opened and will help you fly in the water. In underwater recordings, this moment is perfectly visible, the ankle joint begins to bend in the water, and when the ball kick is finished, the knee stops and the foot continues to move forward. This generates the highest driving torque for leg action in freestyle, backstroke, butterfly and underwater dolphin kicks.

Most importantly, do not teach the kids about the trajectory of movement, do not refer to the mysterious "hip kick", just let the children feel the kissel while kicking a ball under the water.

Now pay attention to how the children move the legs, and in particular the feet, while playing this game in water. As soon as you notice that the feet bend under the water pressure, we can be sure that the children can feel the water on their feet.

---

[1] Kissel is a popular and viscous fruit dish, often served to children in Poland.

The Spinner

The feet already feel the water, so it's time for a spinner. What is that? It is a simple game that, whether you like it or not, forces an effective propulsion of the leg with a small amplitude of movement. Tell the children to:

"Now try to kick the water with one leg to spin backwards."

This is fun because, for the first time, the children will feel the pleasure resulting from the action (kick) and reaction (the whole body is set in motion as a result of the kick). The body spins around, but the nervous system gets a clear message: the movement of the leg with the water sensation on the feet both produce propulsion.

It is important to play this game several times with one leg, and then switch legs; most often, one of the legs will be a bit more effective. This is probably related to the function of cerebral hemispheres, although there is no clear evidence.

All exercises and games must be performed in an upright position with the sleeves on, with the head above the water surface, in deep water.

Okay. The children now have the sense of stability in the water, the water sensation on the feet, legs move optimally in a vertical body position, is there anything else to do? Well... just swim!

Full steam ahead!

The previous games and activities lasted about twenty minutes, and all children whose feet bend under the water pressure when moving their legs can already swim with their feet. By swimming, I mean moving in the water in the direction they want to. Now they just need to properly position their body on the water. Of course, there is no question of immersing the head at this stage – you can skip it for now. The best body position, offering both a sense of security, effective leg propulsion and hydrodynamics, is to place joined arms in front on the surface of water. The arms will form the bow of a ship.

Straight elbows, forearms close together, palms clasped, chin touches the water.

The children are now ready to do their first solo flight in the water, and all you need to do is to say the magic spell, a word that will unlock the inherent skill of all mammals: SWIM!

And they will swim! Alternating movements of legs and the feet that feel the pressure of water will activate the propulsion, the arms stretched forward and the chin in the water will change the vertical balance to slightly more horizontal – this is enough to swim forward. The children swim on their own while still wearing sleeves, holding their head above the water.

Swimming backwards

After this first, so to speak, "virgin" voyage, moving in the water using your feet becomes so natural that you can completely change the body position. The first twenty-five-meter-long swim was enough to understand the action and reaction – the movements of the legs and the propulsion – to realize that "I can swim, it's so easy".

To build on this feeling, tell the children to swim twenty-five meters on their backs. You have the propulsion, now you need to set up the boat. How to do it? The back of the head and the navel are the key points. These two spots, which are very easy for children to locate, should be near the surface of the water. It would obviously be best to immerse the head deep enough so that the swimmer's ears are underwater, but at this point, immersing the ears will be too much of a challenge for many children. Just say:

"Put the back of our head on a water pillow!" And there you have the relatively hydrodynamic bow of a boat. Now focus on the navel position, or specifically the hips position.

With the sleeves on, the children can keep the body close to the water surface, but they will still be a bit insecure and can curl the body up into a fetal position. This is the least hydrodynamic position on the water on the back, but it cannot be eliminated from the start. Why? It's just that everyone has their own adaptive capabilities and the ability to combat fear when performing a brand new task. In this case, the feeling of insecurity is apparent – the more a child is afraid, the deeper they immerse their hips and the navel. You can help a little. When a child swims on its back, gently touch the navel with a thin stick or a swimming noodle (to point to the body part that needs to be lifted), but keeping the hips close to the water surface crucially depends on the individual self-confidence. You can encourage the kids to "lift the navel high", you can use other terms to help them keep the loins and hips close to the water surface, but a relaxed, fully hydrodynamic backstroke position is only possible once they completely let go of their fear.

Regardless of the position of the hips, tell the kids to swim the second twenty-five lap on their backs, encouraging them to look at the ceiling (to help them align the head with the spine). The knees will still emerge out of the water, and the kids will stop every now and then, look around, but they will swim on their own. It could be debated whether the expression "on their own" is the correct term here – after all, they still have sleeves that allow them to float on the water, but at this stage of the training, the most important thing is to teach them the water sensation on the feet and the leg propulsion movements, so the term "on their own" will do for now.

We enter the underwater world

Immersing the eyes, nose, mouth and ears opens up a completely new, unknown world of silence, an underwater reality and inner peace.

For most children, it will be a world of the unknown, and they will not feel at ease here. Perhaps not on the first try – because they trust you and they will eagerly immerse their faces – but most often they will experience quite an unpleasant surprise. As they have not yet learnt to block the nasal septum with air, they will feel water go up the nose into the sinuses, which may cause a short but very unpleasant pain. You all know what I mean – it stings, pinches and hurts so much that you definitely don't want to experience this sensation again. This experience can make children reluctant to immerse their head and face, especially that they can inhale water up their nose and mouth to choke.

However, you can go through this process almost painlessly, you just need to handle it calmly and cleverly.

Preparation for immersion

First of all, do this activity next to the pool, with children sitting at a safe distance from the water so that they can talk freely.

Ask them the following question:

"When we immerse our mouth in the water, how can the water pour into our head?"

The children will probably reply:

"Through the nose, through the mouth, through the ears, through the eyes!"

Reassure them, explaining that:

"Water does not pour through the ears because the entry to the head is blocked. Water does not pour through the eyes because this entry to the head is blocked too, and you have your swimming goggles on. It can only pour in through the mouth and nose. What can we do to prevent this?"

Probably a few kids will come up with the idea of simply blocking their nose and shutting their mouths. Try this. Ask the children to tap their nose with two fingers, as if something smelled bad.

The 5 seconds challenge

Then comes the challenge. The challenge is to inhale air, close your mouth and nose, and hold it for five seconds without releasing any of it. The children keep their breath for a short time, which is enough to learn that, when they submerge their face, it won't hurt them, and it can be fun. Moreover, the breath holding exercise is so short to make sure everyone passes the 5-second challenge test and gains more self-confidence. The challenge is passed.

Full immersion

Now is the time to duck the face under the water for five seconds, just like the Test of Courage.

The children lay on the stomach, perpendicular to the pool, so that only the head is extended above the water surface. They still wear sleeves for safety reasons. They keep almost all of their body on a solid surface to feel secure and confident. Now tell the kids to do the Test of Courage in the same way, but to hold the eyes and mouth closed and plug their nose with the fingers, and immerse the face for five seconds. The children should find it easy-peasy – remember to maintain the safest possible body position because children will try to get up or kneel and be very careful so that nobody accidentally falls into the water. The children wear sleeves and they will definitely stay afloat, but save them the stress.

Once the children can hold their breath five seconds under water several times, encourage them to hold it for seven, and ultimately ten seconds. This is enough since holding your breath for so long naturally causes a mild circulatory and respiratory disorders, or a feeling of tiredness.

Release the nose to get the bubbles

Now it's time to submerge your face without plugging the nose with the hand. And again we may ask:

"Can you breathe out the air through the nose? Imagine you have a congested nose and you slowly blow it out into a handkerchief."

At the beginning, try to blow the imaginary snots very slowly a few times next to the pool, after which do another challenge:

"Who will try to blow the snots for four seconds, but into the water?"

The body position must be safe again to do the challenge. Someone may choke a little, others will ingest some water – but the desire to come up to the task in the newly discovered underwater world will be too tempting to give up. Additionally, there will be air bubbles coming from the nose, so they will definitely have some fun.

The Speed Corridor

The children already know how to keep their face under the water for few seconds, they can block the nasal septum by releasing air, they can open their eyes and look around under the water (wearing goggles). What's next? Well, you should use this skill to teach them how to swim on the belly with the bow of a boat.

Ask the children to enter the water (with the sleeves on) and form the bow of a boat with their arms. An ideal "speed corridor" appears between the shoulders into which they can hide their head. Tell the kids to do this and present them with another task:

"Swim on the stomach with the bow of a boat, and dip your head into the speed corridor whenever you want so that you can see what is happening at the bottom of the pool."

Looking down at the bottom of the pool helps align the head with the spine to help them learn the freestyle, the breaststroke, and the butterfly later on. The body position in backstroke will be the same but reversed, they will look up at the ceiling instead of at the bottom of the pool.

The expression "whenever you want" is important – with these small details, seemingly insignificant terms or phrases, you create the setting of self-confidence, security, and provide the kids with the best conditions to learn new skills. There is a world of difference between "must" and "may". Any compulsion or coercion will only slow down the development of inherent skills, which is the meaning and purpose of your work as a swimming instructor.

What the water tells you – in search for the best head position

Let's go back to the water. Let the kids practice swimming. While doing it, they will now and then look under the water for a few seconds. When holding their head underwater, most of them will definitely feel that their body balance on the water, the hydrodynamics and the swimming speed have improved. Generally, it can be concluded that they have developed the "swimming economics", but it's probably too early to tell – the swimming distances are too short to feel less or more tired. The fact remains that, when swimming with their heads immersed into water and eyes looking down, children will feel they swim "somehow faster and easier".

The term "immerse your head into water" will come up increasingly often. For some children, it will mean touching the water surface with their goggles, nose and mouth. For others, it will mean immersing their head so deep that they can see their feet under the water. The optimum level of head immersion is an extremely important element of hydrodynamics. Where is it? At this and later stages of learning the swimming technique, the best head position is such that the swimmer can look at the bottom of the pool (but not behind), and keeps the ears completely immersed. In a way, keeping the ears immersed, not to deep, just under the water surface, forces a perfect alignment of the head with the spine. Try this:

"As you immerse your head, listen carefully to what the water is saying."

Also, when swimming on the back with the eyes focused on the ceiling, keeping the ears under the water will do exactly the same trick – the hips will naturally rise closer to the water surface and the body position will be more hydrodynamic.

Now swim. What's next?

An experienced politician would probably reply: "Oh, that's a good question, it's a very good question, excellent indeed. Thank you for asking this question." To learn what to do next, let's look at what the kids have learnt so far. In summary:
1. They feel the water (water grip) on their feet.
2. They can instinctively use the water sensation on their feet to create efficient propulsion in the water.
3. They can swim on their stomach with outstretched, straight arms in a "spout" position, keeping the chin close to the water surface or submerging their head under the water so that it aligns with the spine (ears kept under the water).
4. They can swim on their back with the back of the head immersed into water, with the belly and thighs close to the water surface, and arms at the hips.
5. They can breathe out air into the water with their nose (nose bubbles) and mouth.

It may seem unlikely, but children can master all these six skills during the first swimming class. The speed of learning is not a priority, but by working calmly and peacefully, and by precisely following the instinctive swimming method, we definitely increase efficiency and the speed of developing new skills.

Well, to the point – what's next? The children can swim forward, they can immerse the head into water, but they still wear the sleeves. At this point, once again, you need to again remind yourself what you do. You help the kids rediscover their swimming skills by creating safe conditions. These conditions are the sleeves that actually help them overcome their fear. They offer a peace of mind, relative self-confidence, and help develop the water sensation on the feet, and then on the arms.

This is the next stage of your journey into the depths of swimming skills – to boost the water sensation on the palms, and then on the arms.

Hands defrosting

A swimmer feels the water pressure on the palms and arms just as a vehicle feels the road surface while driving on it. The less stable the surface, the more energy is wasted on unproductive movements. An unproductive movement can be defined as a movement that fails to propel you in the desired direction. When you drive into a pool of mud, wet snow, or ice, the engine howls, consumes a lot of fuel, but the wheels that have lost traction keep spinning and the car does not move forward. It feels the same when you try to move through water without really feeling the water on your body.

Without delving into the molecular water structure, there can be no doubt that a better sensation of water pressure on arms creates a more stable, better grip to help you move forward. This is as much true for a six-year-old who tries to perform a simple backstroke drill with one arm, as it is for a twenty-six-year-old who just made the first six freestyle moves at sixty-five frequency in a fifty-meter freestyle final during the Olympics. The success of both swimmers will largely depend on how they feel the stability of the grip with which they move on. Everyone has their own pace, coordination and purpose, but the conditions in water are essentially similar.

The Water-Kissel, part 2

Now invoke the "water kissel" comparison from the drill to activate the sensation of water on the feet. When children are standing in the water (with the sleeves on), instruct them to:

"Immerse one arm so that all fingers are underwater. Your hand is a teaspoon. Try to move your arm so that the water on the spoon becomes thick like a kissel."

Show them this movement, often referred to as "sculling" or "propeller", and pay attention to the palm of the hand to adjust it to the water pressure. At first, children will move their harms to sense the "kissel" also on the back of the hand; your task will be to encourage them to turn their hands in such a way as to feel the water on the palm of the hand as long as possible. When they feel kissel on one arm, repeat the game with the other arm.

Should you pay attention to the trajectory of arm movement under the water in this activity? Present this movement in detail to those who fail to figure out how to make a gentle semicircular arm movement, but the goal is to feel the water pressure on the palm of the hand, and not mapping any specific movement trajectory.

When the children clearly feel the "kissel" on both hands, they should try to find the same sensation while swimming. Again, the children are swimming on the belly, arms outstretched in front and chin immersed. The sleeves on the shoulders will make the children raise their arms a bit unnaturally, but instruct them to:

"Put the teaspoons under the water!"

This is very important because they will never experience water pressure on the water surface, where there is more O_2 than H_2O.

"And now try to feel the kissel on both spoons!"

Children are already familiar with this sensation so they should easily find it again on both hands. It may take some time, but those who feel the pressure of water on one hand will find it while moving both arms. It is important that the children learn to feel the water pressure under the water surface.

For the first time, their arms will experience two distinct feels for the water, supported by the leg propulsion created thanks to the water sensation on the feet. This symbiosis, this specific combination of the two key propulsive forces, will determine the future quality of each swimming style. In the six-, four- and two-kick freestyle, the technique will largely depend on the coordination of arm and leg action, but its efficiency will be the result of the water sensation on the hands, forearms, feet and calves. This also applies to backstroke, which mostly consists of six-kick pattern. In the butterfly stroke, the combination and timing of water sensation on arms and legs in a one- or two-kick pattern coordination at the beginning of a cycle will determine how effectively the arms grab the water as you move your body forward. In breaststroke – where the arm and leg propulsion does not occur coincide, at least in theory – the sensation of when the leg propulsion ends and when the arm propulsion starts will ensure smooth movements and uniform speed. There are many intricacies of the swimming technique, but the propulsive effect of each of them depends on the water sensation, just like the grip of a car tire on the road surface. The water sensation for a swimmer is like a perfect pitch for a musician. The better the pitch, the more beautiful the music. The better the water sensation, the more efficiently, and thus the faster a person swims.

Going back to the pool, the children can already swim using legs only. They put their head, torso and legs quite well in the basic position when learning freestyle and backstroke, and feel the water pressure on their hands and feet.

Jumping into the magic water

It may seem like a crazy idea, but it is best to start jumping into the water during the first class. You can safely do it because children trust you (water is magical and lifts people up, including myself), and you are confident that the children will raise the head and shoulders to a safe position above the water surface within one or two seconds after the jump because of the air in the sleeves and the water buoyancy. You should preferably stay in the water and safeguard the children after each jump, but it is not obligatory. If you feel a child is unsecure, you can give them a stick or any other long and light object to hold on to during the jump at one end, while you grab the other one. At this stage, the children can jump on their feet.

There is one extremely important safety issue that needs to be made very clear. NOTE: Before the jump, tell the children to:
1. Bend elbows and jump into the water in this position.
2. Do not raise straight arms up when jumping into water.

This is the first time you have to be strict as some children may glide into the water with straight arms raised up, which is a very bad habit at this stage of the training. Sleeves can slide off from straight arms raised up when the child hits the water surface. What will happen next is easy to predict: the water will lose some of its magical power, the child will feel stressed. Unless you are already in the water to guard the children, you will have to jump into the water very quickly, almost hearing the heartbeat of a terrified parent watching the scene.

If children keep their arms bent and slightly away from the body when jumping into the water, they will have the sense of stability and they will almost instantly recover the head above the water surface to have access to air.

Jumping at this stage of the learning process adds a great deal of self-confidence in the water. The dynamic immersion of the whole body, head included, for a fraction of a second provides a feeling of complete lack of control over the body, but a moment later the water itself allows you to emerge, breathe in air, and provides a sense of safety. This is yet another invaluable signal for your instinct – water is my best and only friend, it makes me safe. This is a paradox – what threatens you also gives you a sense of security in this very threat (with the little help of the sleeves).

During the first lesson, jumping into the water should be done from the side of the pool, but after a few successful attempts, you can ask:

"Who wants to jump off the starting block?"

Again, "wanting" the key. On the one hand, the children may experience the fear of heights, and on the other hand, they feel the irresistible desire to experiment and explore the unknown. As soon as they start to see, little foxes feel more and more tempted to go out of their foxhole and follow the tiny light at the end of the tunnel that will ultimately lead them to explore a brand new world. This light will be more and more tempting each day, until one morning they wake up and – with hesitation – put their mouths out from a warm and dark foxhole to the vastness of the big world for the first time.

The jump from the block will also be tempting, it will be a challenge. Sooner or later, everyone will jump, maybe someone will dare to do it during the first class? It is enough for one child from the group to do it, the other children will want to join in and follow suit. This is the huge advantage of working with a group of children. The light at the end of the tunnel will become more and more tempting, especially since some foxes have already followed it.

Let's go back to the pool from the foxhole. How long should instinctive swimming classes last? Experience has shown that a lesson should last no more than 45–50 minutes. Of course, this is just a recommendation, but children can get bored when they have to spend more than 50 minutes in deep water. Swimming classes that are entertaining, interesting, engaging should preferably end when the children are still having fun. No one forces you to do anything, only helps. There is nothing better than hearing "Is it really over?" at the end of the class. The children will impatiently wait for the next class, and they will long for something so enjoyable and exciting.

Taking the sleeves off

If the children can confidently swim twenty-five meters on the back, swim on the stomach with immersed head along a four-meter distance, and emerge and swim on the back after jumping into water – without wearing the sleeves – they definitely can swim. After the first two or three classes, most children will be able to do these all of these tasks all with the sleeves on.

Children should slowly get used to swimming while relying on buoyancy, propulsion and balance, but there's not rush. Make sure to carefully watch the children. There are several conditions a child should meet before they can take off the sleeves one by one. What should you pay attention to?

Firstly, when the ankle joint bends under the water pressure during leg action, this demonstrates proper water sensation and effective propulsion.

Secondly, while swimming on the back, children should be able to comfortably keep the position of the abdomen, hips and legs (including feet) near the water surface – the sense of balance and "letting go" of the fear that prompts you to curl the body up into a fetal position.

Thirdly, children can swim on the belly with immersed head for six seconds or more: after taking a breath, they can easily swim four meters, or from the center of the lane to the side of the pool or a rope.

If a sleeved swimmer meets these three conditions, you may encourage them to take one of the sleeves off. Initially, this kind of swimming will be a bit uncomfortable as one side of the body is much more buoyant, which disturbs the overall body balance, but children quickly compensate for this inconvenience by slightly shifting their body position. At this point, you may wonder:

"How is this okay? It forces an unnatural body position!"

Well, you don't need to worry about that. Once the second sleeve is removed, the body balance and propulsion level off very quickly. There is no risk of acquiring "a bad habit".

In general, you may ignore all the dos and don'ts with a clear understanding of the goal you want to achieve. If you want to learn

English, you can choose the Helen Doron method, have conversations with a native speaker, learn in traditional classes, enroll in an intensive course, translate song lyrics – the goal is the same – to acquire the ability to use English. If it turns out that a child starts to acquire a desirable skill or a habit while doing some type of a fun drill or body position in the water, or just by a pure chance, this activity needs to be repeated. You just need to keep your eyes wide open, watch, observe and draw conclusions.

When children start swimming in one sleeve, this definitely boosts their inner confidence that they are able to swim. This is because the sense of security of the magic water is not disturbed – and when one sleeve is removed, children feel they are promoted to a higher level. After this class, many parents will hear their child saying:

"You know, mom, I only swim in one sleeve, it's soooo easy."

What about other children from the same group who do not meet these conditions? Will they feel rejected, left out? Not in the slightest. On seeing that some children were allowed to swim in a single sleeve, they will try even harder to make it into this group.

You may wonder:

"Okay, what are they supposed to do in the water if they can already swim in two or one sleeves?"

They should simply swim. They can swim on the belly with the bow of a boat, looking down at the bottom of the pool for a few seconds, swim on the back with the ears under the water, on the back while clapping hands, swim while standing, make a "kissel" with both legs or spin with one, swim on the belly to make a "kissel" with the arms. "Boats with a bow" can compete in a race (as long as the distance is no longer than ten meters), or do the challenge of making the biggest splash when jumping into the water.

This is one of the greatest advantages of the instinctive swimming method – during the initial stages of acquiring the swimming skills, everyone does the same thing – with two sleeves, one sleeve, or no sleeves. Doing these tasks in deep water helps improve the water sensation, balance, leg propulsion efficiency, and a sense of hydrodynamics, which all come down to swimming.

When to take the second sleeve off?

It's quite straightforward if there is a shallow section in the pool or one long lane in which children can keep their heads and shoulders above the water surface while standing on the bottom of the pool. At the end of deep water classes, move on to the next challenge – tell the children to swim ten or more meters on the back without sleeves. They should keep the back of the head and ears under the water, and the navel and the buttocks in a high position. There is no safety concern – if someone can't do this challenge, they can just stand on the feet whenever they like. Watch the body position on the water while practicing this drill – if the belly and hips are kept high, the legs move effectively close to the water surface and the children can easily swim ten meters, they are ready for their first deep water swim without the sleeves.

Swimming without sleeves

Present this first non-sleeved swim challenge as a task which is even easier than the previous shallow water swimming. In fact, deep water is more buoyant than shallow water, which makes it easier to swim in it (that is why deep swimming pools are "faster" and swimmers score better results). It is extremely important that we assist each child individually – you can do it in the pool or next to it with a stick or a cane, which must be kept close to the swimmer's hand at all times. If the are any problems, try to react before the child completely loses their balance (dropping the legs and hips).

When swimming on the back, the children will hear you despite keeping their ears under the water. Speak loudly and keep reminding them: "Keep the ears under the water!", "Do the water-kissel!", "Keep the belly button high!", "Keep the butt high!". This feedback will give them a sense of security as the fear may kick in again, despite being tamed. If the children become anxious again, they will tend to curl the body up into a fetal position: the hips dropped down, the knees bent, the back of the head elevated above the water surface. The water buoyancy and the balance will be wasted.

How long should this first swim be? There is no optimal distance. It could be five, ten, or twenty-five meters long. It doesn't matter – any body position in the water allows you to swim freely on your back. It is advisable to swim a total of twenty-five meters the first attempt. The children can either take a break (the first swimming interval) or not (the first more serious swimming distance) – all that matters is the final feedback:

"You've swam the entire pool in deep water on your own! Way to go!"

How many classes should a child attend to reach this level? This is something I want to say very clearly at this point – as many classes as necessary to be ready to do it. Most often, several children from a group of twelve begin to master these skills during the second class, and half of the group swims without sleeves during the eighth class. It is quite natural that some children will still swim in one sleeve during the twelfth class. This reflects their individual learning curve. One thing is absolutely certain – at some point they will start to swim on their own. As long as they have contact with water and attend the classes.

If a child can easily swim twenty-five meters without sleeves, can they perform all other drills and activities without sleeves? Not yet. Their first swim without sleeves will probably remain in their memory forever, but they still have to practice a little more until you are confident about their deep water swimming skills without the sleeves.

Swimming on the stomach to a place where you can grab something solid in deep water, to the side of the pool or to a rope is the next important skill. Although the distance will be no more than three meters (the lanes in professional swimming pools are usually that wide), it is a real challenge for children.

The Courage Challenge

"You now need to face a challenge. Try to swim on your stomach with your head underwater to the other side of the lane. There, grab a rope and wait a moment. Then go back along the same path."

Young swimmers will first look at you, then at the rope on the other side of the pool. Even though all children have already swum long distances in this position with their sleeves on, it may now seem a bit far away. Try to present this drill as a challenge done under your strict supervision to make the children feel safe. Swimming on the stomach with the head kept under the water will be super easy, even without the sleeves, if the leg action is effective. The sleeves did not affect the balance, buoyancy, or hydrodynamics. The sleeves were indeed a bit of a nuisance, but were important to keep the children safe while raising the head above the water to take a breath. That's why in this challenge, the children swim to the other side of the lane without sleeves, grab the rope there, breathe for a while in a safe place, and come back along the same route. For you, it will be a clear signal that a child can swim to a safe place on their own, not only on the back, but also on the stomach. After passing this challenge, the little swimmers should repeat it a few times under your strict supervision, but when you see that a child is able to perform this task easily and with confidence, you will get the clear message:

"That's so cool, it's so easy."

Jumping into the water without sleeves

This is another milestone in developing the self-awareness of swimming skills. Before a child makes the first jump, make sure that they understand the following:

"When jumping into to water, make sure to bend your elbows and hold them a bit away from your body. When you come to the water surface, look at the ceiling and put the back of your head in the water. Take a breath and float a bit on your back."

This head position in the water makes breathing easier and helps lift the abdomen and hips towards the water surface. By adding the leg action, a child can quickly become stable once they emerge from the water. Stability is defined as a sense of swimming skills that directly affects the swimming performance. From the very beginning, this sense of stability was the driving force of your cooperation with children, so at this very important moment, the children will almost instantly feel confident about their swimming skills.

During the first jumps without sleeves, make sure to assist the children from the water. They will gain greater self-confidence, and you will provide them with greater sense of security. During the first jumps, you can gently help them emerge to the surface to make up for the missing sleeves. You will be the bridge to the new world. Your help will no longer be necessary after the third or fourth jump; the children will instinctively learn to use the buoyancy of water to reach the surface and your assistance may distract them.

Three levels, one group

If a group of twelve children is trained in accordance with the instinctive swimming methodology, at one point some of the children will be swimming without sleeves, others will swim in one sleeve, and a few children will still use both sleeves. What can be done about it? The answer is clear: you should continue your work. Remember that the instinctive swimming method is designed to develop a natural, individual swimming ability. All the drills that the children perform in the water are geared towards this purpose. The sleeves initially compensate for the disproportions between the safe, free movement in the water and the complete lack of experience of moving around in this specific environment. When this disproportion is levelled off, the sleeves become increasingly dispensable to finally become redundant. All the spins, challenges, jumps, back and belly swimming, and turning water into kissel are done by all children at the same time. The presence or absence of sleeves is the only difference to make up for the disproportions in the group.

Natural born breaststrokers

It may seem surprising, but if you have a vigilant eye, you will be able to spot a natural born breaststrokers already during your first class. You have to watch closely how children position their legs and feet during the first fun activities that help them develop the water sensation on the feet, and how their legs move during the first distances swam on the breast and on the back. There will probably be one or more children in each group who will have a hard time creating propulsion due to the water sensation on the top of the foot. Instead of the freestyle-backstroke leg action, they will repel the water backwards with the sole, gently twisting the ankle joint at the end of the movement. These are the natural born breaststrokers. These children feel the water on the side and bottom of the foot much better than on the foot top, and they do not feel discomfort when performing a semicircular movement (internal rotation) of the lower leg and foot. This is made possible by the specific structure of the hip joint, and more precisely the slightly abnormally longer distance between the head of the joint and the acetabulum on the hip bone. This is why more than a half of all swimmers worldwide do not enjoy the breaststroke very much – they are not able to generate effective propulsion with the legs because of the anatomical constraints. Of course, anyone can learn this movement, but it will always be less effective compared to that in the natural born breaststrokers.

What to do when you spot natural born breaststrokers? Allow them to develop alternate "pre-breaststroke" leg action instead of the freestyle-backstroke propulsion. With this leg action, they will effectively move forward while not standing out from the group. Over time, they will feel slightly higher water pressure on the top of the foot and

will try to generate more propulsion, but they will be guided by the instincts telling them to "spin the water with the side of your foot" instead of "pushing it backwards with the top of the foot". These children will most likely prefer breaststroke swimming and drills over backstroke.

Resting in water

In the instinctive swimming method, floating on the water is not a problem as the sleeves provide perfect stability. However, try to get the children used to floating freely on the back, without any propulsive movements, as early as possible. The most important trick is to teach them to immerse the back of the head in a standing position with the ears kept under the water while looking up at the ceiling.

"And now look at the ceiling, and rest!"

This simple message conveys two of the most important aspects of floating on the water without moving your body. Looking at the ceiling forces a swimmer to immerse the back of the head to obtain the buoyancy necessary to float on the surface. Resting in water means relaxing the muscles, which makes floating even easier.

As you may guess, the resting is done in the same manner in all children, no matter whether they wear two sleeves, one sleeve, or no sleeves. It all depends on how advanced their swimming skills are.

During the first resting in water without the sleeves, you need to carefully watch the swimmers because there may experience a temporary loss of stability in this body position. Most often it is caused by neuromuscular tension, which is a common manifestation of sudden stress. Your fast reaction at this difficult moment will help the child quickly regain confidence, and the next attempt will be much more successful.

When the body is floating comfortably and the back of the head is under the water, the balance in the water will naturally shift from vertical to horizontal. This is not our primary goal in this activity, however, when the body position spontaneously changes from standing in the water to floating on the back, this will definitely be an enjoyable experience because the children will feel the magic water lift their body, and will know you were telling the truth during the first class.

The Balloon

The ability to comfortably float in the water on the back is an unremarkable, but extremely effective and fun activity. Once you practice it with the children, their inner sense of the efficiency of leg action increases significantly. How it that possible?

"Attention, attention, now you will play a balloon. Swim on your back, keep your ears underwater. When I touch your belly with a stick, you stop moving your legs, inhale a lot of air, and close your mouth. You are a balloon now. Keep the ears under the water at all times and just float quietly in the water. I will soon touch your belly with the stick again, then you start moving your legs and swim again. Try to do this several times."

The key moment in this activity is when the leg action begins after floating on the water. This is the essence of effective swimming movements, as if you poured a few drops of hot water into a cup of tea. The body is floating on the water and doesn't make a move, and is then put into motion by leg movements. The swimming instinct then forces the maximum water sensation on the foot; during the first movements, you can see that the ankle joint bends visibly from the water pressure, which means the water sensation is at its peak. The yet inactive sensory proprioreceptors on the foot are "awakened" under these specific conditions.

After the first balloon activity, a careful observer who can recognize the swimming efficiency is able to spot progress in this key element of developing the swimming skills in humans. What do I mean by the swimming efficiency? It can be compared to a simple business rule of exerting minimum effort for a maximum effect. This is why professional swimmers move faster in the water than other people – through training, they can sense this specific point at which the movement and the use of force propels them forward. Beyond this point, any movement is an unproductive waste of energy and generates resistance. In the water, each propulsive movement naturally produces greater water resistance. According to the rules of hydrodynamics, speed is directly proportional to water resistance. In the instinctive swimming method,

the greatest emphasis is placed on the development of swimming efficiency. When you introduce a child to the water environment, present
it a world of unlimited possibilities, in which you can use water to fly
freely. Be patient to progressively develop the sensation of water, then
hydrodynamics, and then the propulsive movement trajectory.

Training progress

In terms of progress, you first need to recall what your training goal is. You want the children to be able to:

1. Feel the water pressure on their feet and hands.
2. Move their legs in the water so that the foot flexes in the ankle joint under water resistance.
3. Float on the water in a supine position with abdominal muscles relaxed, the back of the head immersed, and leg action close to the water surface to swim backwards.
4. Swim forward on the chest with straight arms stretched out in front, head above or under the water.
5. Keep the eyes, nose and mouth under the water for at least five seconds.
6. Not be afraid to swim to the lane rope on the chest with the head immersed and return to the side of the pool from there on the back or on the chest.
7. Jump on the feet into the water from the pool edge or a starting block, swim to the surface and then on the back along any distance, breathing comfortably.
8. The children should master these skills without the sleeves, and should be confident about their swimming abilities.

In fact, the only mark of the training progress in the instinctive swimming method is getting rid of the sleeves. Let me recall once again – you are a facilitator instead of a regular trainer – you create the proper conditions for the children to develop their instinctive swimming skills. A child who acquires the ability to swim and a sense of self-confidence in the water will continue to develop. With each completed distance, the sensation of water, hydrodynamics, and ultimately the efficiency of propulsion movements and the swimming speed will increase.

This very important stage of activating the instinctive swimming skills finishes when a child masters the seven skills listed above. At this point, you may safely declare: this child has recovered their ability to swim, and now they can swim.

Here are some organizational and training tips:

How many children can participate in instinctive swimming classes?

"No more than ten."

Why?

"Because you can easily control that many children in deep water."

Is it possible to hold instinctive swimming classes in shallow water, so that the children can stand on their feet?

"No, because the swimming skills can only be activated in the water, and the whole process will be slower if the children feel a solid ground underneath their feet."

What swimming gear to use for instinctive swimming classes?

"A pair of swimming sleeves for each child, a 1.5-meter bamboo or plastic stick (it can be used to assist swimmers, if necessary), a rubber ball (for preliminary drills to activate the sensation of water on the feet)."

Is it necessary to hold these drills in the edge lane?

"Yes. Direct contact with the children and quick assistance, if needed, are the priority, and this can only be provided in the edge lane. The children will feel more secure when they are close to the edge of the pool, which is important for developing their swimming skills."

Should I stay in the water with children during a swimming class?

"When children enter deep water or jump into water for the first time, they will feel more secure if you stay in the water next to them. However, if you stand next to the pool, you will be able to control and monitor the group and communicate with the group more effectively. You should preferably work in the water during the initial classes, and then stay next to the pool."

How often should instinctive swimming classes take place?

"To be most effective, classes should be held every two or three days."

How long should an instinctive swimming course last?

"Twelve classes; however, some children may need more time to swim in deep water unassisted."

Can this method be used for adults?

"The instinctive swimming methodology has been designed with children and their psychomotor skills in mind. Most of the training elements can be implemented in adult swimming lessons, but different organization and communication approach is required."

Four styles method
Instinctive Swimming

The Backstroke

Style

Through the advancement of knowledge or by pure coincidence, we distinguish four basic swimming strokes, and one underwater swimming stroke, often referred to as "the fifth stroke".

Most people are familiar with these names: freestyle (crawl), backstroke, breaststroke, butterfly stroke, and underwater stroke without a single universal term; most often it is simply referred to as "underwater stroke".

Each style has its own quite, precisely defined sequence of movements, body positions, and the concept of moving in the water.

It may sound controversial, but teaching someone to move in the water in any of the four basic strokes is not difficult. Three basic conditions need to be met:
- effective propulsive leg action,
- sensing the water pressure on hands,
- sense of body balance when swimming on the back and on the chest using only the legs.

In other words, the swimmers in training should simply feel that they are able to swim. If they can swim fifteen meters on the back using only the legs, and a few meters on the chest while keeping the face and ears under the water, we can assume they are able to swim and they believe they do. If these conditions are fulfilled, it should take no more than ten lessons to teach a group of twelve children to swim effectively in one of the four strokes.

Let's embark on a journey to discover the essence of the four swimming styles and to learn how to teach them effectively.

The Backstroke

Classes in backstroke and the three other strokes can be held in both deep and shallow water. You can stay in the water, but to give clear instructions, you should preferably stand at the edge of the pool.

Here, an effective leg action is essential. Without it, you won't succeed. For children who attend the instinctive swimming classes to activate ("recover") their swimming skills, an effective leg action is completely natural.

Of course, you can learn this skill with any other method, but try this simple test at the beginning of your classes:

"Swim half of the pool on your back, keep the back of your head under the water."

If a child keeps their head in the water, the legs are moving close to the surface, and the abdomen and hips form a straight line with the shoulders and the head – you can get down to business.

The Sky

This one short word seemingly has nothing to do with swimming, but it will serve as a signpost to guide the trajectory of movements for those who learn how to move arms over the water.

If a child swims on the back while keeping the arms at the hips, just say:

"Point to the sky with a straight arm!" most children will instinctively make a move along the straightest and shortest path. And incidentally, this is the most ergonomic backstroke movement while lifting your arm from the water.

In this book, I do not use the term "correct" or "incorrect" to evaluate any aspects of the swimming technique. Even though each swimming stroke is defined by both legal regulations and professional literature, it is better to teach each of the strokes based on ergonomics and movement efficiency rather than strict rules. Luckily, what is considered most effective and ergonomic is also in line with the general standards of a given style and the regulations of the World Swimming Federation.

Let's get back to the backstroke. Do you have to bother about the hand position when the arm exists the water? In the instinctive swimming method, it's not worth bothering about. From the moment the arm exits the water until it is lifted perpendicularly to the torso (pointing to the sky), all that matters is the movement trajectory and extension of the elbow joint.

"Show me your elbows!"

All children will now know and feel where their elbow is.

"Extend your elbow, and then point to the sky with a straight arm and then lower it back to the hip."

It is very important that, from the very beginning, the children point to the sky, or hold the arm perpendicularly to the torso for longer than a second, otherwise the body and face will go under the water. This is because the center of gravity will change, and with it, the balance in this body position. This brief second-long pause is enough to develop a movement habit without going under the water. Ask the children to point to the sky with a straight right and left arm alternately. Doing it with both arms at the same time will cause the entire body and head to go down, so should be avoided at this stage.

Although the children will point to the sky with one arm for a brief moment, some will lower their hips and legs. Your task is to remind them to:

"Keep your navel, hips and legs high near the water surface!"

Some may wonder:

"Legs close to the water surface, really? After all, the knees will come out of the water, and this is a fundamental mistake!"

Note that, in the instinctive swimming method, there are no mistakes! The self-imposed chains of limitations will get us nowhere. Your ultimate goal is all that matters. If the kids are unable to move their legs effectively, you should preferably take a step back and work on this aspect. When working with a group, you cannot drastically slow down the progress of the training too often to address problems in one person. You can choose either of the following two options in children with poor leg action:

a)   splashing leg movements with knees coming out of the water, but keeping the balance, with an option to improve movements of the arm over the water in the future;

b)   quiet underwater action of the legs whose efficiency is drastically reduced when an arm is raised, causing an imbalance and drowning.

The choice is obvious and it will not be "the lesser evil" as in Sapkowski's story about the Witcher and his visit to Blaviken. Replacing too high and noisy leg action with more effective movements can indeed take some time, while continuous imbalance and going under the water with "silent" leg action will impede the training process at this stage. Of course, you will feel tempted to use training fins in this and other activities. The problem would disappear, but only in theory. It will most often reappear once the training fins are taken off. Using training fins to develop leg movement efficiency is a bit like teaching a child to play a Western-like piano – the keys are moving by themselves, the music plays, and the child just moves the fingers without making a sound. The fins provide propulsion and movement efficiency, but the child doesn't get to feel water on the feet. As you know, the sensation of water is the essence of effective leg action. So you should not use fins at this stage of the training.

Okay, you've nailed it! What's next? Now you must pay attention to the position of the hands. The best moment to precisely position the hand position before enters the water is when the children point to the sky.

"When you point to the sky with a straight arm, extend your fingers: the thumb points at your feet, and the little finger points at your ears. Then lower the arm back to the hip."

The children will get a lot of new information. However, you need to be precise about the arm position so that the arm goes into the water with as little resistance and as much water sensation as possible. It will make things easier later on.

Ear Base and Air Path

If the children learn how to point to the sky and turn the hand, the arm should no longer return along the same path to the hip from the sky, but continue along an unknown path. This path should lead the arm first to a base at the water surface, and then to an underwater base. The best place for such a base is where the elbow, wrist and hand form a straight line with the shoulder.

Let's now focus on this position to avoid acquiring a bad habit. Unless eliminated in due time, it may cause many problems later and would be difficult to eradicate.

If the arm does not create a straight line with the shoulder when entering the water, and descends towards the head instead, you will get a "virus" that will cause a lot of trouble. The following problems will emerge a bit later – an ineffective water grip, not keeping the torso straight, difficulties in six-stroke coordination and in maintain0ing the continuity and uniformity of propulsion with the arm action. It sounds scary, but this virus can be a real nuisance. If the arm-shoulder line tilts slightly outwards, that's fine. There is a concept of high-performance technique featuring a "wide" immersion of the arm. You have to be very careful that children do not develop the habit of immersing the arm too narrowly.

How can you name this place for the children to understand? On top of that, will the children be able to follow your instructions?

"And now that your hand is turned, touch the base at the water surface next to the ear with a straight arm."

This description may be vague, but it may help the children avoid immersing the arm too narrowly. There may be some exceptions, but the vast majority of children will immerse the arm in a straight line or slightly tilted outwards.

"After you touch the base at the water surface next to the ear, move the arm back to the hip along the same path. Is it an air path or a water path?"

"An air path!" the children will reply.

Although this drill is not designed to practice the arm movement under the water, it will later provide a clear sense of contrast between the arm movement in the air and under the water.

What can the swimmers in training already do?

Let's recap your work so far. The swimmers in training are able to:
- pull a straight arm out of the water,
- move the arm along the most ergonomic path to a position perpendicular to the shoulder (pointing to the sky),
- place a straight arm on the water next to the head in line with the shoulder,
- move the arm back from this position to the hip along an air path

Underwater base

Now the things become really simple. Instead of putting the arm next to the head (ear) on the water, the kids will immerse it a little deeper at this base so that all fingers are brought under the water. If they do, this is where they start to feel the water grip. And if they feel the water grip, it will translate into effective propulsive arm movement under the water. First things first:

"The arm goes by air to the ear base, but the base at the water surface now changes into an underwater base! All fingers must be brought under the water!"

Keep an eye on the trajectory of the arm movement over the water and the underwater base location – it should be next to the ear, in line with the shoulder.

As the arm enters the water, the opposite shoulder can emerge from the water as the shoulder girdle rotates. This is not your training focus at this stage – there is no need to correct this movement. You should react only if the loins and hips start to rotate too much. Why? Unfortunately, if the lumbar spine and hips rotate too much, the children will find it difficult to learn and practice backstroke.

At later stages of training, countering the shoulder rotation with the hips will be an important propulsive movement, but at this point, high hip rotation should be suppressed. This is one of the reasons why all backstroke drills using the instinctive swimming method are performed on the back, never on the side.

Let's return to the underwater base.

"How many fingers do you have per hand?"

"Five!" the children reply.

"Remember that all five fingers must enter the underwater base! When you feel it, go back to the hip base along the air path."

It is extremely important to immerse all fingers – it allows to obtain the best arm position to feel the water and effectively propel the body. Swimming instructors are still in dispute over how the hand should enter the water – some believe you should tilt your hand to the bottom, others argue that tilting it sideways provides the best water grip. One thing is for sure: – some backstrokers tilt their hand to the side to get the water grip, others tilt it downwards.

What is the training hack? At this stage of the training, the sensation of water grip is all that matters, no matter whether the hand is tilted sideways or downwards. When working with a group of ten eight-year-olds, you are not able to meticulously control and correct the hand position in all children. However, we can make sure that the whole hand, including the thumb, is under the water before the children learn to feel and grasp the water. This is the basis for starting an underwater arm movement to generate arm propulsion in back-stroke.

Air Path and Underwater Path

How to teach the underwater arm sweep in backstroke? This movement changes its trajectory three or even four times under the water. Things are relatively simple if you are able to get a proper grasp of water, with no air bubbles in the palm of the hand from the beginning of the propulsion movement.

"And now, when the arm enters the underwater base, you are no longer taking the air path, but – listen carefully – the underwater path!"

The children will now start moving their arms under the water. Of course, it would be best if the underwater arm action was effective from the very start, provided backward propulsion and was aligned with the leg action, but it is hardly possible at the stage. Instead, we can practice this specific movement with simple commands.

In order to boost the swimming efficiency, preferably use the term "arm shift" instead of "arm return" as often as possible. Initially, the term "return" will help children understand the drill, but later should be replaced by the "backward arm shift".

In order to help the children get the best trajectory of the arm movement and arm position during the extension (gliding) phase, explain the following:

"When the arm goes along the underwater path, the fingers must be pointed to the wall of the pool under the water!"

Most children will no longer move the arm under the body with the palm and fingers pointing to the bottom of the pool, which is the most common mistake at this stage of training.

The last remark concerns the final phase of the underwater arm action:

"The underwater arm path finished next to the leg!"

With this piece of information, the children will be able to take full advantage of the sensation of water to effectively move backwards. Some children will then begin to develop a habit to finish off the arm movement (push-back) in backstroke.

Hold on a second, how come you don't teach them the S-shaped movement? Well, you don't. To practice this precise movement would be too much of a nuisance. Rely on your instinct – move the body backwards, fingers pointed to the underwater wall, the underwater path ends next to your leg. That's all you need for the children to place their arm under the water in a grasp, pull, and push sequence.

It's about time to combine these two paths into one smooth movement.

"Now listen carefully, your arm will follow the air path first, and when it enters the underwater base next to the ear, it will return along the underwater path."

It will be nothing more than "one-handed backstroke", a drill often performed by backstrokers. Despite the very short learning time, the children will do very well in a style that is pleasant to look at. Pay attention to a few details:

1. the head is in line the spine, the ears are below the surface of the water;
2. good movement trajectory above the water;
3. the arm is in line with the shoulder as it enters the water;
4. all fingers enter the water;
5. underwater propulsive arm sweep with the fingers facing the wall during the sweep;
6. quiet swimming;
7. leg action with the knees kept under the water surface.

This activity can be done once, twice or thrice, with the right and the left arm alternately. If the children feel confident performing this activity, the next drill – resembling full backstroke – shouldn't be too hard to do.

Taking two paths simultaneously

"Listen carefully, now you will facing a really difficult challenge Hold one arm next to the leg, and the other arm next to the ear at the underwater base, and swim using your legs. Count to three and – that's really important – start moving both arms at the same time. Which path will the arm next to your leg go?"

"The air path!" most children will reply.

"Good! And which path will the arm next to your ear at the underwater base go?"

"The underwater path!" the children will reply.

This short, seemingly innocent conversation will help the children learn how to knowingly coordinate the arm movements in the backstroke. All the previous drills can be compared to atoms that will now form the backstroke molecule. Now you have to correctly combine these atoms. The bond that will hold them together will be to start both arm movements at the same time. It'll be easy for children as they have previously learnt to move one arm over the water, and the other arm under the water.

Why is it so important to start both movements simultaneously? The continuity of arm propulsion is the most important aspect of a full backstroke technique. The most critical moment is when one arm emerges from the water and the other one enters the water, and vice versa. To make it happen without disrupting the continuity of propulsion, one arm should end the air path and enter the water exactly when the other arm finishes the underwater path and emerges from the water. This action should be simultaneous! This is a small yet important detail! It allows to keep the continuity of tactile water sensation and arm propulsion, without any interruption.

Okay, what happens if the children start the arm movement simultaneously? If the children start moving both arms at the same time after a pause of three seconds, they will instinctively finish both sweeps at once. And that's a big accomplishment at this stage of training. Of course, it would be best to perfectly synchronize the moment the arm enters the water and the end of the push-back, but this would only needlessly complicate the training. You'll get to that later, and now make sure the children start and finish the movement of both arms simultaneously.

The next question is where the arm movement should finish after the air path? At the water-surface base or at the underwater base? Well, all fingers should preferably enter the water as they move the arm, but many children may find it difficult in the beginning. This may distort the ability to keep the arm in line with the shoulder as the arm enters the water, which they have mastered before. Therefore, at this stage, all you need is the water-surface base, from which the children have to descend to the underwater base before starting the next passage. It is important that both underwater bases on the right and on the left do not tilt towards the head, which would break the shoulder-wrist-hand line.

After the shift, stop the arms at the bases (by the leg and by the ear), count to three, and make the next shift.

Atom – Particle – Matter

Now the things become really simple. The children have mastered all essential backstroke skills. They have create a style molecule from individual atoms, and are now able to coordinate both arm sweeps. Pay attention to the movement efficiency – the arm sweep also means thrusting the body backwards, in addition to moving the arms in a coordinated cycle. The children should be often reminded about it.

The pauses between the sweeps will slowly bond the backstroke particles – the single arm sweeps – together into full backstroke.

"How far did you count to before sweeping the arms both ways?"

"To three!" the children reply.

"And who will try to make the sweeps while counting to two instead of three?"

Most children will definitely be eager to have a try. Why? They feel they get to the bottom of it and are able to do it. As the swimming instructor, present the pause reduction from three to two seconds as a bid challenge, and the children will be more willing to do it. That was easy!

As you can guess, the next level is a one-second pause, and then a "zero-second" pause.

Hold on a second, perhaps it's better to use the term "no pause"? There is no "zero-second" pause. As a matter of fact, there is. Note that children pause at the bases: next to the leg, under the water, next to the ear. From the very beginning, they were practicing good coordination (starting and ending the sweep simultaneously) and the efficiency of moving backwards during the sweep (the water sensation on the palm once the movement is initiated). The term "zero-second pause" will somehow prompt the kids to enter both bases at the same time, even though the arms will no longer stop there. It may initially seem that the arms are stopping a bit, but over time it will turn into a smooth, effective alternating movement of the arms over and under the water.

To recap, first you create atoms (individual drills), then you combine them into molecules (the arm sweeps with pauses), and finally you create the full style (elimination of pauses) while maintaining all the elements of the backstroke technique.

The Knee-eaters

Although an effective leg action at this stage of training is not your main goal, learning this skill will boost the backstroke skills just like the magic potion brewed by the druid Panoramix provided Gaulish warriors with superhuman strength. Without going into much detail, pay attention to three elements when working with small children: the ankle joint bends under the weight of water, the knees do not come out of the water, and the leg movement finishes when the knee is fully extended close to the surface to create small vortices.

"Did you know that there are birds called knee eaters nesting in the swimming pools?"

"What? What do you mean? Really?"

"Yes, definitely. Look, they have a nest in this swimming pool, over there."

Find a suitable place in advance, next to the ceiling, a lamp, or up on the wall.

"And do you know why these birds are called knee-eaters?"

"No..."

"Because they feed on the knees of children who swim on the back. They wait for the knees to come out of the water and then peck them."

"Whoa..."

"That's true. So if you don't want a knee-eater to peck your knees, you can't push them over the water surface when you swim on the back using your legs. Let's have a try!"

When the children hear this story, you can be certain they will keep the knees under the water, and the leg action will become more effective.

When playing the knee-eater game, children may drastically lower the hips and legs and won't fully extend the legs as they try not to break through the surface of the water with their knees. But fortunately, we have the means at hand.

"Do you know what knee–eaters fear the most?"

"A fire gun! Fire! A wolf!"

"No. They are afraid of the tiny air bubbles that the feet make in the water. They are not afraid of big air bubbles, but when they see small, silent air bubbles above the feet, they run to the nest. Try not to lift your knees while swimming, but also try to scare away the knee eaters with the little air bubbles on your feet."

Creating small vortices (air bubbles) with the feet will naturally create the appropriate amplitude of leg movements and a more hydro-dynamic position of the hips and legs. If the knees do not break the surface of the water, children will be able to produce more efficient leg propulsion during practice and proper backstroke swimming.

Factum est – what the children have just learnt to do:

- Swimming on the back with the head in line with the spine and effective leg action;
- A fully extended arm swings over the water;
- The arm enters in the water with the palm facing outward;
- The arm enters the water in line with the shoulder;
- Arm propulsive sweep under the water with instant tactile water sensation;
- Coordination of above-water and underwater arm sweeps;
- An arm entry into the water is synchronized with the recovery of the second arm from the water;
- Progressive transition from alternating swimming to proper back-stroke;
- Improving the effective leg action by optimizing the technique of propulsive leg movements.

The Butterfly Stroke

The Butterfly Stroke

"What? The butterfly stroke right after the backstroke???" Chris Mannix the Sheriff from Quentin Tarantino's The Hateful Eight asked incredulously.

"Oh, yes," Major Marquis Warren replied, sipping coffee from a tin mug that was not yet poisoned.

Daisy sat quietly and ignored the Major's absurd statement. She stared at a guitar hanging on the wall and remembered the words of the third verse of a folk ballad "Jim Jones at Botany Bay". John Ruth, still chained to her, nervously stared at the faces of the others who had taken refuge from the blizzard in the Minnie's Haberdashery. "Is it possible to teach the butterfly as the second stroke, before the freestyle and the breaststroke?" – thoughts swirled in his mind.

***

We'll never know what was ultimately decided at the Minnie's Haberdashery in Wyoming, during a raging snowstorm. However, there are some facts about the instinctive swimming method as regards the butterfly stroke.

Here's what we know:

1. The butterfly stroke consists of only three main movement elements: the dolphin movement of the whole body, arm movement under the water, and arm return movement in the air.
2. The children quickly learn how to perform these elements thanks to the uniquely transparent training methods.
3. Before all three movement elements are coordinated, they are broken down into clear and easy to connect "bases". As this training largely focuses on the sensation of water on the arms, learning how to breathe in butterfly stroke is not a big challenge for children.

After just one lesson, some of the children can continuously swim two or three full cycles in a proper butterfly stroke. It is reasonable to teach the butterfly stroke so early? By all means, yes – especially since children like learning this style very much, which is the most convincing argument. Let's hit the road to the world of the butterfly stroke to train it using the instinctive swimming method.

The Basics

Just as effective leg action is essential in the backstroke, an effective dolphin movement of the whole body with the arms at the hips, performed at the surface of the water, is the essence of the butterfly stroke.

Again, the term "effective" is what best designates the movements. What does it mean? Nothing other than a movement that makes you move in the water, this time forward. However, the individual components of this movement technique are not as simple as the alternating leg action in backstroke. Of course, some children will very quickly learn how to swim forward with dolphin movements, but others will need some practice. And this will be the first element of the butterfly stroke training using the instinctive swimming method.

Dolphin-snake

The basic structure of the head, torso and leg movement with the arms at the hips is as follows (listen carefully, you have to use your imagination): everything starts with the head, so it goes below the water surface first. As you dive, you look at the bottom of the pool, and the chin is very close to the place where you have a hole at the bottom of the neck, in between the collarbones. As the back of the head goes under the water, the forehead, nose, mouth and chin are facing forward and up. When the face is pointing forward and towards the water surface, the shoulders and the chest go down as if to follow the path of the head that started the whole movement a moment ago. Almost at the same time the hips and buttocks rise and both legs perform a kick simultaneously.

***

"Oh, wait," said Joe Gage, straightening the hat on his head "the hips and buttocks go up because the feet are pressing against the water! That's why they go up!"

"This is absurd!" Oswaldo Mobray said, somewhat impulsively "The downward pressure on the chest forces the entire pelvis upward. I know about these things, after all, I'm the state executioner."

Still warming his hands by the fire, O.B. Jackson began flexing and extending both knees to better understand the essence of the dispute. The giant Senior Bob was touching the suprasternal notch with his chin, then tilted his chin forward and up in an attempt to imitate the initial phase of the dolphin movement.

"Do you have any idea about the structure of the dolphin movement?" General Sandy Smithers waved, getting increasingly impatient with these academic deliberations "The most important thing is to coordinate the downward movement of the chest with the end phase of the kick with both legs. While doing this kick, you have to feel the water on your feet. That's what you should focus on, you miserable bunch of pseudo-philosophers, instead of figuring out what causes what. As the chest and the water-sensing legs are coordinated, the butt has to go up, whether you want to or not."

"Amen!" Major Warren said, and finished his cold coffee from a tin mug. Outside, the wind tried to blow the Minnie's Haberdashery off the face of the earth in a hellish, crazy snow dance.

***

No matter how you approach the dolphin movement, start by cutting the Gordian knot that our friends in Wyoming have tangled up in order to explain and teach it to the children:

And now pretend to be a dolphin-snake. Hold your arms close to the body and try to swim like a dolphin-snake!

Present the movement to the children while standing next to the pool. Pay attention to the movement of the head (the one that Senior Bob tried to do) and the smooth movement of the entire torso. On seeing your presentation, a few children will try to mimic this movement in the water so effectively that they will start to move forward. Their motor imagery, also known as the kinesthetic intelligence, will be their best coach. The chest will be pressed down just after the head descends under the water, the lifting of the hips will be synchronized with the chest going down, and an effective propulsion movement of the legs with the tactile water sensation on the feet will go hand in hand. Therefore, at the very beginning, do not interfere with the motor imagery, just give it a chance to do your job. Have the children practice the dolphin-snake activity.

Why a dolphin-snake, and not simply a dolphin? Most children associate the word "snake" with something long and meandering. Although snakes swim in a side-to-side instead of an up-and-down movement, a snake combined with a dolphin better reflects the nature of the movement and the children will find it easier to imagine it.

Anyway, some children will understand it immediately. What about those who do not? There are two basic things you need to achieve – the leg propulsion and the up and down movement of the head and chest. The hips will then go up spontaneously, as the General Sandy Smithers remarked.

83

Quail Egg and Dolphin's Tail

Play a quail egg squeezing game to teach the children the head and chest movements:

"With your hand touch the small hole under your chin, here [the suprasternal notch]. Imagine that you have a little quail egg attached here, which you must crush with your chin and then lift your chin up.

Do this fun activity next to the pool, uninterruptedly, several times in a row. It will teach the children the initial phase of the dolphin movement."

"Now lie on your belly at the edge of the pool, so that your knees and feet are above the water. Your legs are now a dolphin's tail, join them together and hit the dolphin's tail against the water. Remember to bend your knees, but not too much."

This activity will help the children learn the propulsive leg movement, albeit without the sensation of water, but kicking both legs together is more important at this stage of the training.

"Listen carefully, enter the water, float on your belly, hold your arms next to the hips, and try to crush the quail egg and at the same time make small kicks with your dolphin's tail."

The key is to do it "simultaneously". Even though the two elements of movement are actually done one after another, and not simultaneously, they will start at the same moment in terms of the underwater psychomotor skills of the children. The movement will become smoother as soon as the children feel the water on their feet and keep both knees straight for propulsion. After a few repetitions the children should start moving forward with dolphin-snake movements.

Underwater Dolphin-Snake

As soon as the dolphin movement is relatively smooth, work on the movement efficiency. Use a simple game:

"Swim like a dolphin-snake, but do it under the water!"

When children do this activity under the water, the movement naturally becomes less vertical, its amplitude decreases, and it becomes more effective. Swimming under the water also increases the water sensation on the legs, especially on the feet, which improves the swimming performance.

Kissel – Pudding – Jelly

Start practicing the movement of the arms once the dolphin movements of the torso and legs have become effective. Although this may not be apparent, this drill should be quite easy, provided the kids can feel the water on their hands. Before starting this drill, do a game that the children will enjoy:

"Attention please, place your arms and hands under the water so that your fingers do not come out of the water. Try to thicken the water with the palm of your hand so that it becomes a kissel. Done? Make a pudding out of this kissel now! The water must be even more dense!"

To make the arm sweeps under the water as effective as possible, the children must develop their sensation of water pressure on arms and forearms. To accelerate this process, tell the children to:

"Try to thicken the water so that it is first like a kissel, then like a pudding, and finally it becomes hard like a jelly!"

With this simple game, the children will easily learn how to move forward with butterfly-style arm sweeps under the water.

Two Bases and a Shift

It's time to teach the children how to move arms under the water in the butterfly stroke. However, you won't refer to is as "arms action". Rather, the body will be moving forward across the water with an arm shift.

Ask the children to stand up straight next to the pool or in a shallow water environment.

"Extend straight arms in front of you, so that the hands are opposite the shoulders."

The kids might need some assistance. They don't have to do it very accurately, but make sure that the hands form a straight line with the shoulders.

"Now lean slightly forward and place your head between your arms so that the extended arms touch the ears, and look downwards. This is the first base for your arms."

This fairly precise information on the position of the head and arms should ensure the right balance in the water, which will be important later on.

As soon as the children have mastered the first arms base position, they should now learn to keep it in the water. They should find it easy once they get into the water:

"Put your arms and head at the first base and glide across the water surface on your stomach. Remember to look at the bottom of the pool!

Add alternating leg propulsion after a few gliding movements."

"Now swim in the "first base" position with silent propulsion movements of your legs. Move your legs alternately, like in backstroke."

Now practice the underwater arm propulsion, or the forward shift. Ask the children to stand next to the pool.

"Attention please! Stand up straight and keep your straight arms at your hips and legs. This will be the second base."

The children should easily locate the second base to help them learn how to effectively move arms under the water.

"Listen carefully, now do a special task! Swim with your arms at the first base with leg propulsion. After three seconds, point your fingers down and try to move your body forward with our arms. Your arms should reach the second base at the end of this movement. It has to be done this way."

Demonstrate this movement next to the pool. The movement must be simple, without any additional keyholes or other swirls. Demonstrate the movement with both arms, start with a small bend of the wrists, then run close to the torso with arms flexed at the elbows, down to the hips and legs (the second base). At this point, the movement trajectory is the key issue. What is your main goal?

The goal is to move the body forward as efficiently as possible using the sensation of water on the hands and forearms. Under favorable conditions, the children find the best movement trajectory all by themselves. To create the best possible conditions, make sure to set up the following:

– the first base,

– start of a movement that allows to sense the water (wrists slightly bend);

– the second base,

– body balance provided by the position of the head and the leg action.

To move the body forward as the arms travel from the first to the second base, the children will instinctively find an arm sweep trajectory that suits them best.

After completing this drill, stop, rest for a moment to catch a breath, and do the drill again. Initially, make sure to make a pause after each shift – perform the drills one by one for more accurate and effective practice. After a few successful attempts, suggest repeating the drill twice without a pause – the arms return under the water from the second base (at the legs) to the first base (at the head) after the first sweep.

Shift without the leg action

If the children shift forward without major problems, they should now feel the propulsion from the movement of the arms, without any leg action.

"Swim but keep your arms at the first base. After three seconds, stop your legs and move forward only with your arms!"

When performing the shift without leg action, make sure the children keep the head in a straight line with the spine and hold the torso straight. The children often try to make an additional dolphin movement or dive, which may distort both the water sensation on the arms and the hydrodynamics of the propulsion. At a later stage of the training, the end of the underwater arm sweep will be combined with leg propulsion (often referred to as the "second kick"), but now your priority is to maintain a straight body position.

You may wonder why to sacrifice the precise trajectory of the underwater movement despite an effective water grip, pull and push. Remember that the main idea behind the instinctive swimming method is that the children will arrange their arms and body intuitively to obtain this result. Your task is to create the conditions for it to happen and, if necessary, to put the children on the right path.

Dolphin-snake with arms at the first base

"Listen carefully! Do you want to try making a few dolphin-snakes while keeping your arms straight in front of you at the first base?"

A lot of children will want to have a go. This drill is quite simple, although the arms stretched out in front may have a negative impact on the efficiency of the dolphin movement. To address this, you can use the two drills interchangeably – a few dolphin-snakes, stop and pause, a few breaths, and then a few dolphin-snakes with the arms kept at the first base. Ideally, when performing the dolphin-snake movements, the arms should not go under the water, but the kids may find it difficult and it may reduce the efficiency of this drill. You should pay attention to this technical detail, but leave it for later.

Angel

The butterfly arm sweep over the water is the easiest and fastest to learn, if demonstrated like this, of course.

Ask the kids to stand straight next to the pool.

"Have you ever drawn an angel in the snow? We will now try to make the same movement. Place your straight arms at the second base and relax your fingers. Now touch your ears with straight arms at the first base, as if you were drawing angel wings in the snow with your arms."

Once again, your demonstration will be very important. Make a wide, semicircular movement with straight arms and relaxed fingers. It is very important that the elbows are extended at all times and the fingers are relaxed. It's the shortest pathway from the first to the second base. When the arms are at the head, return to the base at the feet with the same simple movement. After your demonstration, the children should repeat this movement next to the pool a few times, and then go into the water.

Angel on the water

"Now draw an angel in water instead of snow, and you will lie on your belly instead of the back. Keep your head and ears under the water, eyes looking down at the bottom of the pool. Switch on the leg propulsion and draw an angel with your arms on the surface of the water. Not under or above the water, but on the surface of the water."

It only takes a few movements for children to get into the habit of moving their straight arms over the surface of the water. Remind the children to keep the arms relaxed and elbows straight to make sure that the arm sweep from the hips to the head does not end under the water at the cheeks, but on the water surface, preferably above the earlobes.

The Shift and the Angel

"You will now do the most difficult task. Make a shift, and when the arms are at the second base next to the legs, go back to the first base with the angel's wings over the water surface."

"This is very easy!" many children will declare.

"Let's have a try. Arms at the first base, head under the water. Swim for three seconds with leg propulsion, then make a shift and finally the angel's wings return across the water surface to the first base. Remember to inhale a lot of air before starting this difficult task."

If the previous shift drill was effective, adding the return movement of the angel wings to finish the sweep shouldn't be too much of a problem. The position of the head is very important – the head should be in a straight line with the spine, almost completely immersed in the water, eyes looking down at the bottom of the pool.

After several successful attempts, the children are able to perform one full cycle of arm sweeps in the butterfly stroke. Now have them do this drill two or three times without a pause.

"Try adding another shift when the angel's wings return to first base across the water surface."

Everyone should be able to do it without any major problems. Make sure that the children do not jerk uncontrollably to start the shift after the angel's wings return to the first base, but make a smooth movement as calmly as during the first attempt.

"And now we'll do another task. Try to swim the following sequence without a pause: shift, angel, shift, angel. The legs continue to move."

When you explain this task, demonstrate both movements in real time, next to the pool. There is no need to demonstrate it in the pool. During this drill, you may wonder – Holy smokes! After all, they swim using a butterfly arm movement and a freestyle leg movement! This is true, but for now, the children will practice shifts with angels.

As soon as they are able to do two passes and two angels, they can try doing three or even four sequences without a pause – but make sure they do it with the same level of precision.

A lot depends on oxygen supply during the drill, or specifically the release of carbon dioxide when exhaling air into the water. If they do not fully exhale the air after or during the first sequence, they should maintain the relative movement precision while doing more sequences. To help them do it, ask them not to release air bubbles into the water right away. They will learn how to control the inhale-exhale rhythm in proper swimming in the next stages of the training, but they must now memorize the best possible version of this movement and what it feels like.

Do not do more than four shift-angel sequences. Doing more repetitions may lead to cardiorespiratory insufficiency, manifested by uncontrolled, fast and ineffective movements. The children will no longer remember the effective and calm movements; instead, they will memorize violent and unproductive jerks. The training process will become more complicated and time-consuming. It is much more effective to use a series of short drills, each done with maximum precision.

∗∗∗

"There is one thing that puzzles me," said Oswaldo Mobray, playing up his English accent a bit more than usual "How to combine the butterfly stroke movements of the whole body with the water grip? You have practiced these two elements separately!"

"It's simple," muttered the Huge Senior Bob "Make a dolphin as you finish the angel, and you're done."

"Not so fast, my Mexican friend," Oswaldo replied, wagging his finger like a Terminator T-1000 to Sarah Connor "Most children, when told to do so, will do a dolphin too soon before they can feel their arms gripping the water. And yet the secret of the continuous propulsion lies in the combination of the water grip with the arms and the water sensation on the feet, right?"

"You know jack squat about propulsion in swimming," said General Smithers, as irritated as ever "When you sweep your arms over the water, which some idiot called an angel, there's no propulsion. The second kick is over, the first has not started yet, the arms fly over the water. Where is the continuity of propulsion, you English fool?"

"Hold on a second," said Sheriff Mannix "In the dolphin kick, the feet move back and down to move the body forward, don't they?"

94

"Yes," All eight responded in unison after they came together during a snowstorm raging in Wyoming.

"When the arms start grabbing the water, should the dolphin kick start or finish?" Mannix continued his investigation.

"It should be finished, of course," Daisy said, trying to tune her guitar's G string at the same time. "The legs make you swim with the highest speed, which can be maintained by starting the water grip and by continuing the arm sweep under the water, which this idiot refers to as the shift. Right, Johnny?" she asked as she played an E minor chord on a perfectly tuned guitar.

"Oh yes," nodded John "The Gallows," Ruth appreciatively, "When one ends, the other begins."

Poison and caffeine were already mixed together in a blue kettle on a small stove. Outside the Minnie's Haberdashery, you could hear the wind wailing a song about the upcoming death.

Dolphin-snake – Shift – Angel

Based on this lovely exchange of thoughts on the biomechanics of the butterfly stroke, try doing a drill that brings together all the elements that you have practiced so far in the previous drills. What is it about?

First, you need to ensure the initial body balance: arms at the first base, head under the water. A short glide on the water surface and two dolphin-snakes with the arms held at the first base. Begin the shift as you finish the second dolphin-snake. When the body moves forward and the arms are at the second base, finish it off with an angel whose wings return across the water surface to the first base. Once you learn this sequence, leave only one dolphin-snake, which is immediately followed by a shift, and then an angel. A piece of cake.

Traps

You will come across the first trap when doing the dolphin movements with arms in front, at the first base. As you move your head and chest down, your outstretched arms at the first base will also begin to plunge deep beneath the water surface. Encourage the kids to avoid this movement:

"When we do the dolphin movements, the first base must not go under the water!"

Don't expect the children to perform this drill very precisely, because the arms and shoulders of the dolphin movement will always go under the water a bit. However, if the immersion is too deep, it will definitely limit the quality of the water grip later on, and the dolphin kick and the initiation of the propulsive arm sweep will be combined in an unfavorable manner.

The second trap shows up during the shift phase. The kids very often perform an uncontrolled, additional dolphin kick while moving their arms under the water, which has nothing in common with the so-called second butterfly kick. This disrupts the forward propulsive movement and this habit will be is hard to eliminate.

"Remember to straighten your back during the shift!"

This remark should effectively eliminate the unnecessary dolphin kicks during the forward shift.

The third trap for those who practice the butterfly stroke is the attempt to dynamically and uncontrollably sweep arms over the water during the angel movement.

"Before the angel begins, straighten its wings (elbows) and loosen the feathers (arms). Remember that the wings glide across the water surface, not over or under the water!"

If the angel's wings come into contact with the water surface, it will help balance the body position and prevent jerky movements. As the kids progressively learn to do this drill more effectively, the angel's wings will travel more and more over the water rather than across the water surface, but initially, the arm sweep must be made across the water surface.

The final trap is holding the arms too long at the second base after completing the shift and before starting the angel movement. When the underwater arm sweep has finished at the second base, tell the children to start the angel movement immediately. It is true that, in the beginning, a brief arm pause at the thighs allows to straighten the angel's wings, but there must be no pause between the shift and the angel.

That's it?

Well... yes. The dolphin kick, immediately followed by an effective forward shift generated by both arms, and finally a wide, smooth return movement of both arms across the water surface. It's important to keep the body balance, head immersed, hips close to the water surface. This is the "by-the-book" butterfly-stroke cycle. What's next? The next cycle, preferably identical and made immediately after the angel returns to the first base. And what's next? Another one, if you still have some air in your lungs. This is the butterfly stroke.

Okay, but what about the breath?

***

"It's a mistake to teach the kids to raise your head to breathe as late as in the last phase of the underwater arm sweep," Major Warren said as he sat down at the table with a bowl full of hot stew.

"I've heard a lot of new theories today in this Haberdashery, but it's not a theory – it's a freaking training nonsense, Marquis Warren," Mannix said impulsively, with a strange satisfaction in his voice. "Haven't they taught you, dear bounty hunter," he continued "that when you grab water and pull, you have to get the most hydrodynamic position of the body?"

"So what?" asked Joe Gage, intrigued, and put his hat on the wooden table.

"So you can't teach anyone to raise their head, because that creates resistance and your hips go down!" said Mannix triumphantly. "This is only allowed during the final phase of the underwater arm sweep. Your theory is rubbish, you arogant clown."

Warren continued to eat his hot stew. Mannix's provocative words seemed to make no impression on him.

"Sorry boss, the major seems right," Oswaldo joined the conversation with his usual smirk "Breathing indeed begins in the last phase of the underwater arm sweep, but you need to get into this body position to take a breath. Raising the head to take a breath takes just as long as it takes to grab the water and pull."

"So what?" asked Warren, kind of agreeably.

"So the head movement to take a breath must begin simultaneously with the underwater arm sweep, which some idiot called a shift!" General Smithers exclaimed from his chair, "That's not a fantasy of some clown in a Union uniform, just plain reasoning!"

Major Warren rose from the table. He approached the stew pot and placed a hefty portion into the empty bowl next to it. He walked over to the fireplace where Smithers was sitting.

"Can I join you?" he asked the General and placed the smoking bowl next to him.

"

Breath

Believe it or not, learning to breathe in the butterfly stroke is not that hard. It takes little effort to lift the entire face (the forehead, eyes, nose, mouth and chin) above the water surface during the shift – the water sensation and hydrodynamics are all that matters. And it just so happens that we have already practiced both of these elements earlier. However, you need to start with teaching the kids the head position over the water while taking a breath.

"Listen carefully! Is it possible to breathe through the mouth when the bottom of the chin touches the water? Let's find out."

The kids must be able to stand on the bottom or next to the pool to have full control of the immersion depth of the chin. When they find out they can actually breathe with the chin in the water, try to combine the underwater arm sweeps with the movement of the head to this position. Timing is the key, as discussed at the Minnie's Haberdashery.

Note! Now comes the most difficult part. Try to do two things at the same time: move the legs alternately to do the shift and raise the head out of the water to see what is happening on the other side of the pool.

These instructions are too vague to perform the drill correctly, so this is a more detailed description:

"Set your arms at the first base, put your head under the water and swim, alternately moving your legs. Count to three and make a shift with your arms. And now the most important thing – at the same time raise your whole face above the water to take a breath. And when you take a breath, stop."

After the first attempts, try to synchronize the head and arm movements, according to Major Warren's theory:

"Remember to start lifting your head the moment you start the shift, not a second before, not a second after!"

If the children begin to move their heads to the water surface and sweep their arms under the water at the same time, they should be able to take a breath exactly as they finish this movement. This is the best breathing moment because of the body has the highest acceleration, and the raised head will not force the hips down too much. That's not all – at a later training stage, the second kick will be performed at this point, which will boost the hydrodynamics of the entire body position. In this drill, the alternating leg movements is your greatest ally to maintain the high hip position. Of course, in the next training stage, these movements will be eliminated, but now the freestyle-like leg action is very helpful.

At the initial stage of the training, the kids should pause after each drill performed, rest for a while, and perform the drill once again. After several cycles, when the head and arms movements are sufficiently coordinated to breathe comfortably, instead of a pause, you can add an underwater arm sweep from the second base to the first one, and then start the next "breathing action".

Breath and Angel

As you might imagine, the next step will be to practice return movement of the arms over the water after taking a breath. However, to keep
the balance, the kids need to develop the habit of placing the head under the water after taking a breath, when the angel's wings start flying
to the first base. The choice of this moment may be controversial, as
professional butterfly swimmers put their head under the water just before the end of the above-water arm sweep. However, you are now training children who only learn how to feel the water and synchronize
the butterfly stroke movements. To recap:

"When you take a breath, your head has to go back into the water,
and when it does, the angel's wings return to the first base!"

There are two simple drills to combine individual elements into a
uniform movement that you will one day refer to as: "butterfly arm sweep and freestyle leg action, breath taken every cycle". At this point, the
kids will understand it as a shift with the head raised to breathe and
then hidden under the water, followed by an angel movement. Take it
easy, be precise, do not rush.

Dolphin-snake – Breath with a shift – Angel

The final step in practicing butterfly breathing is to eliminate the freestyle leg action to replace it with a single dolphin-snake movement. Make sure to use the concepts that the children are familiar with – dolphin-snake, shift, angel, etc. The kids will easily understand the next drill – the only serious challenge now will be to effectively perform the individual elements of this activity. And right now the efficiency of the dolphin movement and the shift will be crucial as you want to eliminate the continuous leg action and replace it with just one dolphin kick.

"Now you will have to face a very difficult task. Turn off the alternating leg action and do the following sequence: a short shift, one dolphin-snake, and a shift with a breath. After that, stop and rest for a while."

In this drill, some children will still use a bit of freestyle leg action to make taking a breath easier. However, once the swimming becomes smoother and more effective, the alternating leg action will fade away. In fact, some children will spontaneously develop the second dolphin kick.

The final step is to add the angel's wings return movement to first base coordinated with the head immersion. A piece of cake.

Developing smoothness

When all atoms and molecules merge to provide full coordination, the kids will swim forward in a way that can confidently be called a proper butterfly stroke. However, as you will easily notice, they will still lack the desirable smoothness of movements. There will be two pauses – one at the first base, before making the dolphin-snake, and another one at the second base, after making the shift, and before the angel movement.

First, let's eliminate the pause between the shift and the angel.

Angel Launcher

Stopping the arm sweep at the second base (at the thighs) after the shift has so far been necessary in order to develop the full, effective arm action under the water. In order to smoothly combine the end of the shift with the start of the "angel" movement, play a launcher game to teach the children to immediately throw the arms forward across the water surface from the second base.

"Let's play a launcher game. Move the legs alternately, keep the arms at the first base for two seconds. Make a shift without taking a breath and without an angel. Instead, set up a launcher for angel wings at the second base. This launcher needs to go off as soon as you are done with the shift, you don't stop your arms at the second base anymore."

Some children will be so concerned not to stop their arms after the shift that they will stop the underwater sweep halfway. In this case, remind them that the launcher is placed at the second base, not under the chest. However, don't pay too much attention to where this movement should end, because it may distort the whole task. Preferably, tell the children to:

"Start thinking about the launcher when your arms are near the navel."

This will help them smoothly do the underwater-to-overwater arm sweep.

Cycle Connector

The next task will be quite challenging, because it will teach the kids to coordinate the end of the overwater sweep (angel) with the dolphin kick (dolphin-snake) and the start of the shift. For swimmers proficient in the butterfly stroke, these movements are done almost simultaneously – the arm arrival to the first base is synchronized with the beginning of the dolphin kick and the beginning of the water grip. This is obviously too difficult for the novice swimmers, but you can easily teach them to instinctively sense the good coordination of the moment, namely by shortening the pause between the end of the angel movement and the beginning of the next dolphin-snake movement.

First name and Surname – First Name – No Name

"Try this drill: dolphin-snake with arms at the first base, shift, and an angel with a launcher. Don't stop the movement when you finally land at the first base, just say your first and last name in your head, and then make a dolphin-snake, a shift, another angel, and then stop."

Shorten the pause after several successful attempts:

"Okay, and now do the same, but say your first name only instead of your first and last name!"

The last step is to eliminate the pause almost completely:

"Now do the same, but when the angel's wing land at the first base, do not repeat your name or surname, immediately do the dolphin-snake when you land at the first base, and then a shift."

Here's a trap – some children will cut corners and start the dolphin-snake in the middle of the angel movement. This will obviously disrupt the timing and efficiency of the movements (Oswaldo Mobray mentioned it at the Minnie's Haberdashery), so we need to remind the kids to start making the dolphin-snake movement only once they feel the angel's wings have landed at the first base. After combining the two cycles smoothly without a pause for the first and the last name, add a third or even a fourth cycle.

In all these drills – with a pause for the first and the last name, the first name only, and without any pause – the head should not be lifted for breath. Once the kids have become proficient in this task, add the breath, preferably every second or third cycle. This will allow the kids to make more repetitions, but add the breath only if you are confident that both the cycles and their combination are performed smoothly and effectively.

Small distances – high efficiency

Now that the children have mastered the proper butterfly stroke, you must not be tempted to let them swim longer than ten to fifteen meters. Note that your current goal is to develop stroke efficiency through the sensation of water and the appropriate coordination of the movement of arms, legs and torso. Despite the ability to repeat the movement sequences, a seven-year-old child will become weaker with each meter, and the swimming performance will worsen. Therefore, at this stage of the training, you should allow the children to swim short distances to maintain high efficiency appropriate to their age. Over time, the swimming distances will be extended from ten to fifteen meters, then twenty, and finally twenty-five. Take it easy! A seven-year-old swimmer will hopefully continue to swim the butterfly stroke for at least seventy more years, and they have plenty of time to master 200 meters butterfly.

Scales and Passages

Like in any other swimming style, each individual drill will develop the overall efficiency of the butterfly stroke. After learning to swim short distances with full coordination, during each class use any selected fun activities that you have practiced before. Dolphin-snakes, angels, shifts with or without breathing – individual combinations of drill can be compared to playing scales and passages while learning to play an instrument. The aim is to learn to play individual pieces of music more smoothly and with greater mastery. Thanks to fun activities, the children will gradually master the butterfly stroke.

Factum est – what happened here a moment ago

- Coordination of the movement of the head, torso and legs in the butterfly stroke;
- Effective swimming in the butterfly stroke;
- Improvement of the water pressure sensation on the hands;
- Effective underwater arm sweeps in the butterfly stroke;
- Wide and low movement of straight, relaxed arms across the water surface;
- Head in line with the spine during arm sweeps under and above the water;
- Coordination of the dolphin kick with the start of the arm sweep under the water;
- Coordination of the end of arm sweep under the water with the start of arm sweep over the water;
- Coordination of the end of arm sweep over the water with the start of the dolphin kick;
- Synchronization of the arm sweep under the water with the lifting of the head for breath;
- Learning the low head position during breathing;
- Coordinating the breath end with the start of arm sweep over the water;
- Coordination of the dolphin kick with the end of arm sweep over the water and the beginning of the arm sweep over the water;
- Combining individual cycles into a smooth swimming style.

Freestyle

Freestyle

"Do you really think that, if you teach the freestyle using the add-on method, the children will keep the sensation of continuous arm propulsion?" Lieutenant Vincent Hanna from the movie "Heat" by Michael Mann looked deeply into the eyes of Neil McCauley, both sitting at one table for a quarter or two. The roadside bar on Highway 309 was bursting with visitors that evening, but the two men seemed to be indifferent to all other people surrounding them.

"Yes, I think so," said Neil, calmly but firmly.

"Look, bro," Hanna said, "if you give me one piece of evidence, one freaking scientific proof that add-on is better than a kayak, then maybe I'll agree with you."

McCauley tilted his head slightly towards his left shoulder and replied:

"Hydrodynamics."

"Hydrodynamics? That's all? Is that your proof?" there was a hint of irony in the lieutenant's voice, though deep down he had real respect for Neil.

"Yes. And now I will ask you a question," McCauley said calmly, "Will a six- or seven-year-old who has just learnt to swim be able to synchronize six-stroke leg action with kayak-like arm movements?"

Hanna said nothing, just stared at Neil as if to penetrate his soul.

"You know well they don't. It's going to be a broken two-stroke crossover, or God knows what. At this stage, the long line formed by the legs, torso and arm is more important than the sole continuity of the arm propulsive movement without rhythmic leg action. You would otherwise get ineffective jerky kayak-like movements across the water surface."

Hanna smiled almost imperceptibly.

"Okay" he said without any trace of anger "okay."

***

The conversation of these two gentlemen very clearly outlines the concept of learning freestyle using the instinctive swimming method. First, the hydrodynamics of the body position, and secondly, the generation of propulsion. High swimming speed at this stage of the training doesn't matter at all, but learning the habit of hydrodynamic body position will translate into effective propulsion in the future. Dear Reader, if you want to sail on the endless waters of the freestyle practice, make yourself a good tea, add some rum, and let's embark on this journey together.

Head, head, head

Or to be more specific, the head position. This is the beginning of the story. If the children attended swimming lessons or learned the butterfly stroke with the instinctive swimming method, they will naturally position their head in a straight line with the spine. If this is not the case, this is where you start.

What is the correct head position? After all, when you watch Thorpe or Phelps freestyle racing on YT, they both look forward, while sprinters, for example, position their head perfectly in line with the spine. As for women, it's hard to find any regularity at all. For example, Sarah Sjostrom puts her head in line with the spine, and Ranomi Kromowidjojo looks forward and doesn't keep a straight head-spine axis. All these comparisons will get us nowhere. It's a bit like trying to teach a child to play the piano without being able to choose which winner of the Chopin Competition to look up to: Seong-Jin Cho, Rafał Blechacz, Kristian Zimerman or Bruce Liu?

Speed Corridor

For children learning the freestyle instinctively, the hydrodynamics and body balance will be the top priority. Therefore, the best head position is where a straight head-spine line is created. How to instruct the children to do it in a precise and effective manner? Ask everyone to stand against the wall and lean their backs against it.

"Lean against the wall, look forward, and touch the wall with the back of your head. Now touch your chin. Do you feel that your chin does not touch the hole at the bottom of the neck [suprasternal notch], but is away from it? Now lean forward so that you can see the floor. Listen carefully, keep the same distance between the chin and the hole at the bottom of your neck!"

Some children will change the head position in relation to the spine when they lean forward, so help them with it. Correct the body position, and remind them to keep the distance between the chin and the hole.

"If you keep your head in the same position in the water, the head will be placed in a special speed corridor. This will make you swim faster."

Speed Corridor and First Base

Now ask the children to stretch their arms forward and put them at the first base. Those who have learned instinctive butterfly swimming will be well familiar with this body position. All those who are just starting their instinctive swimming adventure will have to learn it now:

"Stretch your arms forward so that your palms are opposite the shoulders."

Some children may find it difficult to align the arms with the shoulders, and make corrections if necessary. Move on once everyone has the correct body line.

"At the first base, there is a speed corridor between your arms. Lean forward and place our head in it as we did a moment ago, but keep your arms at the first base. Remember to keep the distance between the chin and the hole at the base of the neck!"

Because all the small details you have been working on so far, the children will find it easy to find the proper body position. However, if they don't, assist the children to get to this body position as it will soon be very important.

Leaf on The Water

Go into a shallow section of the pool or a place where you can stand on the bottom of the pool. It is mandatory, but the children will not be breathing at the beginning of this drill, so they will have to make a pause every now and then. Of course, this activity can be done it in deep water with a breathing pause at the edge of the pool or the laneline, but it is more convenient for children to stop while standing on the bottom of the pool.

"What happens to the leaves in the autumn?"

"They fall from the trees!"

"That's right. And when a leaf falls into the water, what happens to it? Does it sink or does it float?"

"It floats!"

"Correct. Now you will play leaves floating on water. Note! With your arms at the first base and the head in the speed corridor, look down at the bottom and slide on our belly on the water surface, just like the leaves in the autumn!"

After a few more or less successful attempts, add a few details that will help the children work on the body balance. These are:

1. arm immersed a few centimeters below the water surface;
2. relaxation of the cervical muscles;
3. placing the head so deep under the water that the ears are fully submerged.

If the "autumn leaves" float high in the water during the glide, with hips and legs touching the surface, and only a part of the back of the head is visible above the water – you can add the leg propulsion.

A leaf with an engine

"Attention, attention! Now each leaf will have a water engine on its tail. What can that motor be?"

"The legs!" the children will reply.

"Correct. Now let's play the game of leaves with an engine. Make a leaf without an engine in the water, and when you feel that the leaf is already gliding, add an engine, or leg propulsion. When you run out of breath, stop and rest for a moment."

In the beginning, the moment of gliding without arm sweep is necessary to establish the body balance and high body position in the water. If you add the leg propulsion too soon, the previously established body position can be slightly distorted, so it is better to activate the propulsion after one or two seconds of gliding.

***

There was a large bottle of Heinz ketchup standing in the center of the table where the policeman Vincent Hanna and the thief Neil McCauley were sitting. It was this red bottle that McCauley was staring at, trying to find a counter argument to what Hanna had just told him.

"You're speechless, ha? This is what it's like when you think you really know it all, and suddenly it turns out you know nothing at all." The lieutenant's eyes seemed to be smiling, though the rest of his face was dead serious.

"A better over-water arm movement translates into a better arm entry into the water and a more effective water grip," Neil finally said. But the ruthless confidence disappeared from his voice.

"This is all true, but as I told you a moment ago, the arm movement over the water is the least important part of the freestyle training" Hanna replied calmly.

"Or do you also think it's not worth to teach it?" Neil asked and smiled a little mockingly.

"No, but only after you learn the body position that will allow you to move your arm freely over the water. Then you teach the propulsion movement of the arm under water. Only when the kids learn to do it, you add the arm pull back movement over the water. And let me tell you, brother, the training will be fast, easy and fun," Hanna said and smiling, his dark brown eyes widened.

"Okay," Neil replied, with his usual composure, "okay."

Shift

"Listen carefully! Who wants to try to swim a three-second leaf with an engine and then make a forward shift with both arms underwater?"

"Me, me!"

"That's not all. As you move forward, the head cannot leave the speed corridor, even for a split second. Shall we try?"

In this short conversation, you ask the children to combine two very important elements of the freestyle stroke: effective forward movement with the arm under the water while maintaining head in line with the spine. It's okay if you do it with both arms at once. As you can easily guess, the children will soon be asked to do it with only one arm, but the propulsion without lifting the head will be invaluable.

"Who will try to do the same with just one arm? Keep the second arm at the first base in the front!"

During this exercise, pay special attention to the position of the arm in the front. In theory, the task is simple – the arm position should not change when the other arm remains underwater.

"As you move forward, the other arm remains at the ear, and the fingers are pointing at the wall in front of you!"

This should help keep the arm in front of you in the correct position.

Shift - Return - Shift

"Now let's try something more complicated. After you move forward on one arm, do not stop. The arm that was making the shift will now go back under the water to the first base! Is it difficult?"

"Noooo, it's easy!" the children will reply.

"That's not all. When the arm is back at the first base, the other arm will start moving to make a shift as well. Only then can you stop. Who wants to have a try?"

This is how we start the add-on game that the Lieutenant Hanna questioned.

Rotation / Rolling

How to tackle the topic of torso rotation in freestyle training?

In the instinctive method, rotation is not a training goal itself. It is a natural alignment of the shoulders and torso during the propulsive movement. The kids learn to make effective forward movements from the very beginning, without excessively lifting one or the other hip up. There may probably be discussions about the relationship between hip rotation and the efficiency of forward propulsion, so I will now make a clear statement:

Teaching an expensive, almost ninety-degree freestyle hip rotation is a serious training mistake. It negatively affects the efficiency of forward propulsion during underwater arm movement.

Unfortunately, despite the best intensions to learn the children a streamlined torso position, they learn to sway from one side to another, which inhibits the forward propulsion in both phases of the cycle.

Okay, if you're so smart, how can you teach it without affecting the propulsion?

Tunnels

Ask the children to stand straight in a place where the water is shallow.

"Imagine that there is a special tunnel under the water in which you place your arm when making a sweep you have learnt to do; we called it "one arm". This tunnel is straight, not too deep, but it does not touch the surface of the water."

Here, for the first time, you begin to learn the front arm position, which is crucial for body balance in freestyle. At this stage of learning the freestyle, the wrist position at the shoulder depth is not yet precise, but now we will work on the underwater position of the arm, and specifically the hand. Try lowering the shoulder from ear to cheek.

"In order for the arm to be correctly positioned in the tunnel, lower it a bit at the beginning. Stand straight, place your straight arm so that your arm is against your ear. This is where the tunnel begins. Now lower the beginning of the tunnel on the cheek. Remember to keep your arm straight!"

Second arm

After this first, fairly simple exercise performed next to the pool, add a second task:

"Now try to do this: when you lower the beginning of the tunnel to the cheek, fold back the other arm. Remember to keep your head still and not move it when you do this movement!"

Present this movement to the children as they may understand the expression "fold back the other arm" differently.

This is how you kill two birds with one stone: rotation of the shoulder girdle and arms, and arm position at a gentle angle to help balance the freestyle.

When the children master this movement next to the pool, try to perform it in water:

"Attention, attention! Swim like a leaf with an engine for three seconds, and then make a one-handed slide. That's not all. When doing the slide, lower the beginning of the tunnel on your cheek with the arm that is left in front, and swing the other arm towards the ceiling."

This exercise is crucial to the entire freestyle, so take the time to learn to do it precisely. You need to work on four elements during the slide:

1.	a steady, non-lifted head position with the gaze focused on the bottom of the pool;
2.	keeping the arm in front in a straight line to the shoulder;
3.	lowering the shoulder of the arm remaining in front to the cheek;
4.	raising the other shoulder above the water;
5.	continuous leg action.

There is a lot to learn, but working on these elements will pay off. If the children learn how to perform these elements precisely, to the best of their abilities, we will create an extremely effective propulsion basis for the freestyle cycle. Everything we do after that will depend on its quality. Keep your eyes wide open and devote as much time and attention to your pupils as they will need to master these five elements in a single-handed movement.

Is it possible to teach the precise trajectory of arm movement under water? Of course you can, but when working with the instinctive method, encourage the children to perform the propulsive movement forward with their fingers pointing to the bottom. The time will come for learning a high shoulder position during the grip, early extension of the forearm, inswip (putting the elbow to the body at the end of a stroke) and other technical details. Now all you need to do is the water sensation and effective forward movement.

Shark

This is the name for the body position after the slide. Once the kids reach this stage, encourage them to keep swimming in this position for a while. This is the basis for all other training activities, getting a sense of balance will determine the quality of the following exercises. Useful tips: a straight line-spine line, looking down at the bottom of the pool, ears immersed entirely under the water, the leading arm (in the front) a few centimeters below the water surface, arm of the leading arm touching the cheek under water, the opposite arm remains above the water surface (rotation), effective and continuous leg movements. That's a lot, beg your pardon for the Proust-like sentence. Once you have found your way through this long sentence, my dear Reader, and if the kids are able to comfortably swim in this position for a few seconds, it's all downhill from here in the freestyle training.

What about the hips? Do not rotate the hips too much but at the same time, do not prevent the rotation. Try to find the most comfortable shark position. Instead, react if the children rotate the hips ninety degrees or more – it's definitely too much, so you have to intervene:

"When swimming in the shark position, the navel must not look at the top part of the side walls of the pool, only at the center or bottom of it!"

This should help achieve a hip position that is optimal for the body balance. Of course, some children will be so preoccupied with the body position that they will completely eliminate the rotation of not only the hips, but also the torso and shoulders – watch the kids closely and help them gain a sense of balance and freedom to swim in the shark position. If the head and the leading arm are at the proper depth, the shoulder girdle and arms are rotating, and the hips are slightly juxtaposed against the shoulders, and that's fine.

Breath

Neil watched calmly as Vincent Hanna twisted his head to the side, trying to rip it off with a arm movement that imitated a water grip in the freestyle stroke. The lieutenant was doing it so discreetly that the guests gathered at the bar on Highway 309 seemed hardly interested.

"So you want to teach your kids the correct freestyle breathing just because they have found the correct balance in the shark position? You know that this is the hardest part of the training. Why the hell teach them something beyond their grasp?" Hannah asked, irritated.

"And why the hell did you teach an effective leg action before? All those tunnels, corridors, shifts? Why is this awesome basis for balance and efficiency in the shark position so important?" Neil spoke softly but firmly. "To make the next training stages as easy as possible, right?"

"Of course, but trust me, learning to breathe is extremely difficult. Raising the head, drooping the hips, leaning on the arm, immersing the mouth; have you not heard about it in your mysterious world?" Lieutenant Hanna no longer hid his sarcasm.

"Of course I did. But when it dawned on me that the freestyle breath was just a head twist to the side and adding a slight hip rotation in the shark position, everything has changed. The problem is that the foundation for balance and efficiency is too weak, not the breath." Mccauley said smiling discreetly. When he finished, Vincent Hanna remained quiet, just looked intensely into Neil's narrowed eyes. Finally, he took a breath through his mouth as if to say something, but then gave up.

"Don't say anything, just focus on the balance and leg action with the shark, the rest will be easy peasy. Okay?" Neil asked calmly and cheerfully.

"Okay," Hanna replied.

Three points

To teach breathing in the freestyle stroke with the instinctive method, you need to combine three elements: the head position, the high hip position during the breath, and effective one-handed shift. Let's start with the head position.

"Do you think it is possible to breathe by mouth when one cheek, the side of the goggles and the side of the head are touching the water?"

Instead of answering straight away, most children will begin to wonder if this is actually possible. Remind them that side of the goggles and the side of the head (i.e. the part above the temple) must touch the water in addition to the cheek. When everyone is comfortable doing this exercise, raise the bar:

"Do you think it is possible to breathe when one cheek, the side of the goggles and the side of the head not only touch the water, but also sink a little under it?"

They will again start wondering whether it's possible. During these experiments, ensure that the side of the head – the part above the temple – is submerged under the water while keeping the chin at the water surface; this translated into an optimum head position in line with the spine. Of course, do this drill on the right and the left side.

We've nailed it! Now teach the children to use the shift to turn the head for breath. Just like in the butterfly stroke, start both actions simultaneously. Many people may wonder why, as the breath must come after the arm emerges from the water, so the head twist for breath will take place at the end of the underwater sweep, instead at the beginning. Well, dear Reader, when practicing breathing, this concept is of no use. Due to the loss of speed (breathing takes place after the end of the arm propulsive movement), the hips drop, the head is raised, and a straight head-spine line is broken.

In the instinctive method, you use the shift energy for the head twist for breath to get the sensation of high body position, especially the hips. At this exceptionally hydrodynamic moment (the body is in motion thanks to the underwater action of the arm, hip and leg at the surface of the water), it is easy for children to inhale the air on the side. All they have to do is slightly increase the torso rotation and twist the head to the side without lifting it up. If the temple, the side of the goggles and the cheek are then submerged, they will be able to breath in air through the mouth. And now we go to the heart of the matter: if you want the breathing to begin at the end of the arm action under water (and this is your goal), the head twist leading to that breath must begin when the arm enters the water. If this happens later, the breath will coincide with a loss of shift velocity, when the hips will drop, and this will force the children to lift their heads for air. This will open a tiny box of Pandora's bad breathing habits in the freestyle stroke. How do you avoid opening the box? The answer is quite simple: when you start the shift, start to twist your head as well.

Two journeys

"When your arm starts the shift, it goes on an underwater journey. The same goes with the head: when you start to move it to take a breath, it also goes on a journey, but into the air. Let's try to start these two journeys at the same time."

First, practice it next to the pool – two arms in front, head between the arms, and when starting the movement of one arm down and back, start a gentle movement of the head to the side. Focus on this moment – the head is to start turning exactly when the arm starts to move, not before and not after (this is the timing that Lieutenant Hanna mocked in his last conversation with Neil). Note – when moving the head to the side, let the children breathe out through their noses. This habit will naturally develop in the course of time when practicing in water, but make sure the children start learning while practicing next to the pool. The children will not experience the unpleasant and painful feeling of water pouring through the nose.

"Let's try to do what follows: a leaf with an engine for three seconds, and then a shift with one arm, and the head and arm pathways. Remember to start the arm journey under water simultaneously with the head journey to the surface, which we have practiced before. When you feel your mouth come out of the water, you can take a breath."

"And when I take a breath, what then?"

"When you take one or more breaths, you can stop."

The children will start to modify this exercise, so pay attention to the following: both journeys starting simultaneously, the head turns but is not lifted, the arm in the front does not come down. You can even say that the arm in the front supports the back of the head – this will help the children get into the habit of extending the body line as they breathe. To facilitate breathing, encourage children to look at the ceiling when turning the head – to help them avoid lifting the head and the mouth should have better access to air.

Return pathway and another departure

"Listen carefully! Try not to stop after taking a breath. Instead, return to the leaf with an engine. Both the head and the arm go along the same path, under the water!"

This won't be very challenging, and the kids will learn it very quickly. Remember the children to return their head to the underwater speed corridor.

"And now, once your arm returns, count to three and again follow the same path to catch a breath, only to the other side. Then go back as the leaf with an engine. You can try this several times without a pause!"

This is how to learn the children rhythmic breathing in freestyle.

Shift - Shark - Return - Shift - Shark - Return

The very title of this section indicates the nature of this exercise. Let's have a try!

"Once you return from the shark to the leaf, not to stop, but make another shift to the shark, but on the other side. Take a deep breath to have enough air for the entire exercise!"

All this action must be done without breathing in order to get the best possible hydrodynamics. To recap: two seconds of a leaf with an engine, a shift and a shark, an underwater arm return action to the leaf position, a shift, and a shark on the other side. Pay attention to a few technical details during the shift and the shark. Head movement without head lifting, moving the shoulder of the arm in front on the cheek while lifting the other shoulder above the water, continuous and effective leg action, keeping the arm in front in line with the shoulder. Why do I keep repeating it over and over again? The quality of freestyle stroke is at stake.

Cheek stop

When the children have mastered the transition from one shark position to another, it is time to say goodbye to the leaf movement as a means to join both arms in the front. Start learning the children how to make a shift in which both arms will move together for a while. However, this exercise will also keep the core muscles working, which was previously a matter of fact.

"Listen, we can now move from leaf to shark, go back to leaf and do shark shift again. And now, after you make the first leaf, you will not let the two arms in the front come together. The arm return action in the water will stop halfway. It's a cheek stop because it's next to the cheek. We'll stop there for two seconds. Now focus: when the arm at the cheek stop moves forward after this short pause, the other arm will not wait for it anymore, it will start to move at the same time. Let's try this while standing."

It may seem a bit complicated, but it will become easy after some practice next to the pool. Your task will be to make sure that, once the arm stops at the cheek stop, the movement of both arms starts simultaneously. This is the first time that you eliminate the add-on that Lieutenant Hanna was so afraid of. However, the hydrodynamics and the activity of the trunk muscles during the shift will be maintained.

Enter the water after a few exercises next to the pool.

"Do you remember what to do? Swim like a leaf with an engine, make a shift and shark, return the arm to the cheek stop, and make another shift from there!"

In the beginning, many children will first move their arm from the cheek to the front anyway and will only then begin to the shift, but remain vigilant and correct it so that everyone learn the correct timing. As a reminder – one arm is against the cheek, the other one in the front in the shark position, and at the same time both arms begin the shift to the next shark.

What about breathing? For now, it won't be needed. Of course, you can add it, but only when the children are able to correctly perform at least three shifts. In these three repetitions, you can develop correct coordination freely without bothering about the breath. Remember – it is not the distance covered during these exercises that matters, but the quality of performance.

Overwater arm movement

Neil was shaking his head in disbelief. What Vincent had just said was beyond his comprehension. Despite all the experience, knowledge and openness, McCauley could not, simply could not agree with Hanna, even to some extent.

"Listen to me carefully," he said, "it will never work. You can't teach anyone how to move an arm over the water without actually teaching it! This, my dear colleague, is a training whim that is destined to fail" he concluded and took his last sip of cold coffee.

Hanna stared at him, his wide-eyed eyes glittering.

"Who said anything about teaching?" he said finally with a smile. "Just don't intentionally position your arm. Not doing all those freaking zippers next to the torso, the elbow angles, wrist folding, so it doesn't touch the water. It's all a waste of time."

"Mr. Brilliant Policeman, can you tell me how to do it?" asked Neil, mockingly.

"As naturally as possible. If you have a good balance in the shark position and you move one shoulder above the water, the rest is effortless. Teach the kids to move a relaxed arm out of the water with an elbow pointing up. Not too high, let the hand stay in the water. Then slide your fingers across the water surface to the leaf position. It will be a spontaneous action."

"Maybe yes, maybe no," Neil still had his doubts, although what Hanna had said about balance and shoulder was pretty convincing.

A hole in the sky

"Listen to me, let's do something funny when swimming in the shark position. Let's make a hole in the sky!"

"What? What do you mean?"

"How do you think we can do this?"

"With a stick! With a gun! With a rocket!"

"Or maybe try your elbow? Swim for two seconds as a leaf with an engine and make a shift to the shark. Swim for two seconds as the shark and relax your fingers. Then raise an elbow up to make a hole in the sky. Not too high, relax your fingers and you may keep your fingers in the water. Once you make a hole, hide your arm. Shall we try?"

Remind the children to constantly relax your arms already during their first attempts. When the arm emerges from the water, it will naturally move towards the head if the hand remains in the water. During the first attempts, it will return from this position back to the leg and hip, but once the children master this exercise, the arm return movement to the hip will be replace by a forward movement to the first base, i.e. the leaf position.

Shift – Shark – Hole in the Sky – Leaf

"Look, after we make a hole in the sky, try not going back to the hip, but move your arm forward, to first base, instead. Do you recognize this movement?"

"A leaf!"

"That's right. Let's try, just remember that the fingers should be relaxed all the time and should not come out of the water."

To recap: two seconds of a leaf with an engine, a shift and a shark, then a hole in the sky, and finally put the arm back to the first base. The secret of overwater arm action consists of two elements: the elbow pointing to the sky, and relaxed fingers gliding across the water surface. Note that the shark position, which you practiced earlier, is where you put one shoulder above the water surface. The overwater shoulder action forms a kind of key that opens the way for the arm. Just raise the elbow up and the arm starts to move forward. Make sure that the arm freely slides across the water surface next to the body, without touching the torso, during the entire exercise. This will ensure freedom of movement and will help keep the balance and position of the torso in the shark position. Okay, when the arm emerges out of the water, the body is in the shark position. How long should you keep it? Throughout the overwater arm action? Do not waste your time on this tiny detail when children learn this movement, it will only complicate the entire drill. Children who want to make a hole in the sky with their elbows are unlikely to drop the shoulder, and that's a lot. In the next stages of the training, when the add-on will turn into a freestyle stroke, you will focus on the high shoulder position with the correct timing. For now appreciate the high elbow in the first phase of the movement and the relaxed arm glide across the water surface.

Do this drill on one side and then on the other. At the beginning, after one repetition, stop for a short rest, but then try to perform two or even three repetitions without pausing for a breath.

Can you breathe in instead of a pause and continue the drill? Preferably not. Take a moment, let the muscle memory remember some of the most important details before interrupting this process with your breath. A breath that forces you to reposition your head, increase rotation, and can still go wrong. It's better to pause after three or even four repetitions, rest for a while, and start the drill again.

Dragon

Driving relaxed fingers across the water surface while pointing the elbow to the sky creates the freestyle movement of the arm over the water. Once this movement has been mastered and the children are able to switch comfortably from one shark position to another, it's time to remove the fingers from the surface of the water while maintaining the structure of the movement. For this to work, divide the arm pathway over the water into two parts – the first part remains the same, i.e. fingers across the water surface and elbow in the sky. When the arm is next to the head, take your hand out of the water for a moment, as if to jump over the obstacle, and place it under the water in the final phase of the movement, all the way to the first base. But is it still an instinctive, simple and natural form of movement? After all, children have to precisely perform as many as three elements in this one, short movement... But don't worry about it. You only need a short story about a dragon.

"A tiny dragon lived far, far away. This dragon loved the water and used to sit by the ears of swimming children. But he didn't like it when the children ran their fingers over him while practicing their freestyle. It turned red and breathed fire. What can we do to avoid having your fingers burnt by the dragon?"

"Jump over it!"

"Yes, that's what we'll do. When your arm glides across the water surface to the first base, jump your fingers over the dragon next to the ear and move it calmly to the first base. Then do the same on the other side. Shall we try?"

Make sure that the children take their arms out of the water only near the ear. For the time being, it is necessary to develop the arm movement over the water while keeping the shoulder and the elbow high.

Children often worry so much about the dragon that they take their fingers out of the water right away, pointing the elbow backwards rather than upwards. This arm position causes an imbalance and limits the action of torso muscles in full-style swimming.

Hasta la vista, here we go again with the add-on

"You brought it up yourself. I must admit you have taught the kids to beautifully move their arms over the water. But they have also learned that, when one arm moves above the water, the other arm is idle and waits. They will always have an add-on in the freestyle stroke. Do you want all the children in the world to become long-distance swimmers?" Vincent Hanna mocked in a familiar way "Even professional freestyleers," he continued, "those naturally swimming the FQS (Front Quadrant Swimming) technique do not wait with an idle arm in front of them in a so-called glide. When one arm comes out of the water, the other arm slowly grips it to keep the drive." Hanna was talking so emotionally that all the guests from the next table looked in his direction for a moment.

"Take it easy, everything is thought out and planned." Neil spoke very quietly to calm Hannah down and avoid the attention of other guests. "Do you remember the stop next to the cheek?"

"Yes, I do, so what? It was a completely different drill," Vincent Hanna spoke calmer now.

"Not true, my friend. It was an identical drill, but now the arm goes over the water – as you taught the children to do, not under the water. The kids will pause at the cheek stop, and then do two things at the same time: jump over the dragon to the first base and start the shift," Neil smiled. He already knew he had convinced Vincent.

A hole in sky and a cheek stop

"Who remembers the cheek stop? Try to pause at the cheek stop while making a hole in the sky with your elbow. Then go back to the hip and leg along the same pathway. Do what follows: a leaf with an engine, a shift and a shark, and then a hole in the sky, go to the cheek stop with relaxed fingers gliding across the water surface, touch it, and return the arm to the leg and hip."

This drill is to prepare a kind of "reloading base" to change the synchronization of the arm actions from additive to alternating. Make sure to maintain the extended body line by extending the leading arm. In a more professional nomenclature, you will be learning the kids using the front quadrant swimming technique, or FQS.

There is one detail to pay attention to: when the children touch the cheeks with their fingers, the center of gravity will move forward. If they remain in this position for more than one second, they will start to drown. Unfortunately, it is inevitable, so encourage them to touch the cheek stop and move their arm back immediately. In order to activate the trunk muscles and keep the balance, another important thing is to point to the sky with the elbow while touching the cheek. Some children will forget this and will then point their elbows backwards – thus they might learn the habit of keeping the arm above the water with the arm in front and a low elbow behind.

"Remember, when you touch your cheek, your elbow is pointing to the sky! This should help."

"And now do not go back from the cheek stop to the leg. Instead, do the shift and jump over the dragon. Just a note, it has to be done simultaneously: when the shift begins, the fingers on the cheek jump over the dragon to the first base. Not sooner, not later, but at the same time."

The children already know the timing – they learnt it when practicing how to combine the shift and transition of the arm from the cheek to the first base under the water. The arm position that touches the cheek is the only difference – as Neil McCauley noted. The arm used to be immersed, now the elbow is making a hole in the sky, so it's almost entirely over the water. The coordination of arms, legs and torso action is the same in the forward shift. This is why they used to practice all the sharks, tunnels, stops and holes in the sky, so that now there would have no problem doing this exercise. Exercises performed on both sides without a pause will include a full freestyle cycle, broken down into two small pauses: the shark position and the cheek stop.

Of course, in the early stages of practice, it is better to do just one pass and stop. After a few successful attempts, encourage the children to do this exercise on both sides without any pause. They can even do it several times in a row.

You may wonder whether this exercise includes breathing. Again, the answer is – preferably no. At least not in the initial stages of training. It would be much more advisable to perform this exercise several times without any twisting movements for the breath. If you run out of breath, stop, rest for a moment, and make a few transitions from shark to shark again. There will be time to integrate breathing into the exercises.

A vanishing stop

The final step in learning freestyle with the instinctive method will be to eliminate the short pauses that used to be an important part of each previous exercise. The pauses organized the exercises, helped the kids to think about what they were supposed to do now, and to recall small technical details. The most important pauses took place were as follows: the first pause – when the shift was over, before taking the arm out of the water; the second pause – when the fingers touched the cheek stop, before jumping over the dragon. First eliminate the cheek stop.

"Look, I have important information for you. The cheek stop is gone. The arm pathways is the same, but there is no more stop, so it cannot pause there. Who wants to try to make a few shifts like before, but when you make a hole in the sky, do not stop at the cheek anymore, just go past it and jump over the dragon right away. Let me remind you once more: when one arm jumps over the dragon, the other is already starting the shift!"

You won't find it difficult, you are soon to be professional freestyleers. Perhaps they may still be a little confused about the timing of the arrival – some will perform an add-on as they begin the shift once the arm gets out of water, others will do a kayak fan, because they will start the shift too early, before the arm reaches the cheek level. However, these inconsistencies are very easy to identify and eliminate. Just keep reminding them to:

"Start the shark-to-shark switch when the arm jumps over the dragon. Not later and not sooner."

Elbow Launcher

It's high time to eliminate the pause after the shark-to-shark switch. Play it smartly so that the children do not finish their movement too early, but do not finish the movement at the thigh level without any propulsion.

"Look, there's an elbow launcher at your hip. When you use it, you will no longer stop your arm there after a shift, but immediately take the elbow up to make a hole in the sky and go to the dragon. Shall we try?"

To tell the children that the launcher is at the hip is a clever way to keep the shift power, and at the same time to eliminate the unproductive water-pushing movement backwards at the thigh. Keep all other synchronization elements as in the previous exercises. Everything is running smoothly and a little faster, and there can be several transitions as long as they are performed as precisely as possible.

Breath at least

Only now, when the nervous system has learned to coordinate the movements of arms, legs and torso as well as the body position on the water, you can confidently introduce a head twist to breathe during the shift. If the children trained it well before (that was your goal), the rhythm and coordination throughout the exercise should not be drastically affected by breathing. Of course, children will take two or three breaths instead of one quick breath at first, but when they get used to it, encourage them to take one breath only. And, of course, alert them that the head must return to the speed corridor after a breath.

How often to breathe? It would be best to breath on both sides, i.e. every third move, however, this may not always be the case. Breathing will always be easier and more comfortable on one side, and children will preferably choose this side. However, entourage them to practice breathing both to the right and to the left to develop and coordinate both shifts at the early stage of training.

Toe-eater

"Do you remember the knee-eating bird?"

"Yeah, he pecks the knees as you stick them out of the water in backstroke!"

"And did you know that toe-eaters also live in swimming pools? They feed on the toes of children who put their toes high above the water in backstroke."

"Whoa..."

"That's true. Luckily, they are also afraid of the foam that the feet make on the water. Let's try to scare them away with this silent foam."

Note that the freestyle leg action is effective when the top of the foot (where you have your shoelaces) is in constant contact with the water. As long as the sole only slightly cuts the surface of the water, the loss of efficiency is negligible. If, on the other hand, the entire foot emerged above the water surface, it creates a downward movement that impacts against the water surface instead of a propulsive movement.

The best position to naturally boost the leg action is to swim on your belly while keeping your head out of the water. However, it requires both strength and some efficiency of the leg action, so preferably do not use it at the early stage of the training. Instead, in the beginning, use the imagination of the children who have just learnt about the toe-eater.

"Attention please! Swim like a leaf with an engine, you may keep the head in the speed tunnel, but it's not necessary. Raise your toes high above the water, but scare away the toe-eaters by making a little foam in the water with your feet. Try not to stop for a breath, just raise your head above the water and breathe while swimming!"

Raising your head above the water for breath will force your legs to move even more efficiently. You will now be able to hold this position for a brief moment, but over time you will be able to do it longer.

You can remind the children about the toe-eater when doing pre-freestyle drills and full stroke drills.

Factum est – what happened here a moment ago

- Head in line with the spine;
- Balance in a breast glide, with arms stretched forward;
- Effective leg propulsion in the balance position on the chest;
- Underwater propulsion of the right and left arm by grabbing, pulling and pushing the water away;
- Swimming in balance, high rotation of the shoulder girdle and low rotation of the hips, with one arm stretched forward, while remaining at a depth that helps keep the balance;
- Head position in line with the spine as you breathe;
- Synchronized head tilting to breathe with the underwater arm movement;
- Rhythmic breathing in the underwater add-on with one arm;
- Underwater add-on with the right and the left arm in a more pronounced rotational position;
- Alternating movements under the water in a freestyle-like synchronization of the arm action;
- Low elbow position when the arm comes out of the water;
- Running the arm above the water with a high elbow position, relaxed forearm and fingers across the water surface in an add-on drill;
- Running the arm above the water with a high elbow position in an add-on drill;
- Running the arm above the water with a high elbow position in an alternating movement drill;
- Combining the cycles into a proper full stroke;
- Adding rhythmic breathing on the left and on the right side for a full stroke;
- Improving the effective leg action by optimizing the technique of propulsive leg movements.

The Breaststroke

The Breaststroke

"It can't end well." said Gimli from Peter Jackson's "The Lord of the Rings" movie. "Every dwarf whom I taught the breaststroke leg movements, first thoroughly and patiently practiced the whole movement while lying on the ground, then in the water and then also lying down! What you are talking about is simply impossible, you're just being presumptuous."

Legolas stared at the burning torch that lay slightly away from the fire.

"Tell me, dwarf," he said without taking his eyes off the fire, "What is the biggest difference between breaststroke and other styles?"

"All of it," Gimli muttered.

Aragorn, who stayed out of the conversation, smiled. He lay with his arms behind his head and watched the starry night sky.

"But if you had to choose something," Legolas insisted.

"The legs. I would choose the leg action." Gimli said.

"Exactly. And what is the biggest difference between the leg action in breaststroke and other styles?" Legolas looked away from the fire and stared into the narrowed little eyes of the dwarf.

"The fact that the propulsion is created by the sensation of water on the side and sole of the foot, rather than on the top of the foot. Or didn't they teach you that over at your Elvish schools?" Gimli said cheekily.

"They did," Legolas answered calmly. "They also taught me that you won't feel water unless you are in it."

"So what?" asked Gimli.

"The legs in breaststroke will be well positioned only when the side of the foot and the sole feel the resistance of the water," Aragorn joined in, still lying with his arms behind his head. He was looking to the north side of the sky, at the Andromeda constellation. "Therefore, it is better to teach it only briefly next to the pool, and continue with the training in the water."

"This insidious alliance between elves and humans will not abolish the thousand-years-old dwarf training tradition," Gimli grunted.

***

Whether you agree with Legolas or the "thousands of years old dwarf training tradition" – there is no breaststroke without the frog legs. To be more precise – without the sensation of water on the side and the sole of the foot, the legs will not generate the propulsion, which is the key to breaststroke. It is true that in professional breaststrokers, the arm action can be more important than the leg action, but this applies to a completely different training level. In your training, almost everything depends on the efficiency of the leg action, so it needs to be your priority. This does not apply to the natural born breaststrokers you may remember from the previous section – can do it straight away, like little frogs that have just morphed from tadpoles.

The letter L

"Stand up straight and look at your legs. What is the letter created by your foot and the lower leg?"

"The letter L!"

"That's right. Now stand on tip toes as high as possible. Which letter is it?"

"The letter I!"

"Good! When you swim backstroke, butterfly and freestyle, did were your legs arranged in the letter "I" or "L"?"

"The letter I!"

"Correct. Now forget the letter. The most important thing right now is the letter "L"."

This is crucial to getting started with the breaststroke leg action according to the instinctive swimming method. Despite the most sincere intentions, children will not feel the water on the side and bottom of the foot, if the foot will be parallel to the tibia before the kick. The children will tend to keep the foot in this position because of the memory of the nervous system – propulsion is the sensation of water on the top of the foot. Small circles, foot abduction and other tricks won't help – the propulsive movement will be ineffective.

"Put one heel up towards the buttock, but the foot must still remain in the letter "L" position. Then do the same with the other leg."

Pay attention to two things: first, it is the heel should go up towards to the buttock, not the knee towards the belly. It is easy for children to control this movement next to the pool, so keep an eye on this element. Second, many people unknowingly shift their foot position from "L" to "I" when lifting the foot. This is the point of this game – to get into the habit of lifting the foot to grasp water in the "L" position – so watch it closely and correct it if needed.

Extending the feelers

When the foot is correctly lifted towards the buttock, twist it to the outside. Let's call this movement "extending the feelers".

"Now we'll do something truly different. Once you raise the letter "L" towards the buttock, twist it outwards so that the fingers can see what is happening on the side. It will be a feeler that will soon feel the thick water. Then lower the foot down. Let's try: raise the letter "L", tilt the feeler to the side and put your foot back on the floor."

Do this drill while standing, not lying down, as we will be doing it in the water in the same position.

Do the same in the water

"Let's find out if you can do the same in the water. Hold on to the rope with one or two hands and try to raise the letter "L" towards the buttock in the same manner as you did next to the pool."

This drill is done in a vertical position. Your goal is to create the sensation of water on the foot, but only to raise the heel towards the buttock as the knee is bent, with the foot in the "L" position. In other words, teach the children to make this move in the same way as they did next to the pool a few minutes earlier. They can try with one leg, but it will be easier to do it with both legs at the same time.

Floating on the feelers

After a few successful repetitions, add the opening of the feet – to extend the feelers – and the return movement downwards in the open position. During the return, if the foot is in the letter "L" position, a propulsive movement will be initiated. Reinforce it by asking the children to lift the body up during the return movement.

"And now, when you lift the letter "L", extend the feelers and try to lift yourself up on them!"

"Lift it up" - this is the key to success. You don't have to demonstrate the semicircular movement, or teach any propulsive trajectory. This is the essence of what Legolas talked about – the sensation of water will be your greatest ally. Of course, it would never worked out hadn't we practiced the "L" position next to the pool, raising the feet and extending the feelers first. These drills prepared the children to correctly perform this seemingly most difficult element without much effort. Do this drill while holding a rope or the side of the pool. However, if you see that the return movement of the feet causes the body upward movement, encourage the children to try to do this drill without holding on to anything while keeping the arms along the body.

Smiling Knees

Children will often spread their knees wide while raising their feet, extending the feelers, or just the return movement. This will make the propulsive movement ineffective, so you must respond to eliminate this undesirable movement. You will need a waterproof marker for this.

"Stand straight. I have a special marker here that will make my knees smile."

Now draw eyes and faces on your knees. Children will enjoy it and smiley face will soon be very useful.

"Who wants to have the smiling knees?"

A few children will surely come forward, give them the marker pen and ask them to paint eyes and faces on their knees.

"And now we have a special task: when raising the letter L, extending the feelers and the return movement, the smiling knee has to look forward all the time, it cannot look to the side. Let's have a try!"

Go to the water after a few repetitions next to the pool.

"Raise your body as you did before, but now remember about smiling knees! They must look forward all the time, they can't look sideways!"

Of course, it's okay if the knees open a little before the propulsive movement, but make sure that it does not interfere with the efficiency of the return movement of the feet.

Leg propulsion

"What are you going to do now, elf?" Gimli asked. He failed to mask the deep satisfaction in his voice. "You may have taught them the leg position and an effective kick, for that matter. But all this was done standing, with the torso and thighs in a straight line! There is no such position in the proper stroke or even in swimming with the leg action only!"

"Gimli is quite right, Legolas," Aragorn spoke, "With the breaststroke kick, the thighs break the straight line with the body, it's the only way."

"Why are you so concerned about this?" Legolas asked, "When the standing position changes to a reclining position on the belly, the thighs will naturally bend at a slight angle to your torso."

"Are these some Elvish stories straight from the forest waterholes?" the dwarf was indignant "If you put your head under the water, your hips will touch the water surface. And if that is the case, the feet will come out of the water before the water grab to catch air instead of the water, or worse things will happen; to avoid this, the knees will go under the belly, which will completely eliminate the propulsion! Everything you've learned in a standing position doesn't make sense in a horizontal position," Gimli almost shouted.

"Aragorn, do you remember when you visited our forests of Lothlórien, and you saw elves swimming," Legolas addressed Aragorn.

"Yes, I especially enjoyed watching the little elves swim while keeping the head over the water, without using their arms," Aragorn responded "It was as if they were bouncing from the bottom every now and then, and yet the forest ponds of Lothlórien were over thirty meters deep. I have never seen anyone swimming like this before."

"This was the next stage of the training," Legolas replied, "leaning the body forward and using the trained leg action to swim forward."

"With the head above the water?" Gimli asked mockingly, "After all, the head position must be hydrodynamic, otherwise there're won't by any glide!"

"When dwarves are swimming the breaststroke, how do they keep their head when they pull up the feet? Over the water or under the water?" Legolas asked calmly.

Gimli set a huge shield aside, on which he rested his arms and head. He got up and began imitating the breaststroke movements. His arms, head, and one leg could be clearly seen in the light of the fire, moving synchronously. When he inhaled, he paused with a foot lifted.

"Over the water," he quietly replied to Legolas. There was no trace of certainty in his voice.

"If the head is above the water, the legs will catch the water more easily when you tilt the feet outwards," Aragorn argued, "This is why the little elves were swimming so dynamically in the elvish ponds… they had excellent sensation of the water grip in breaststroke leg action, and were not bouncing from the bottom," he said, looking at Legolas.

"I always say, grasping the water with your feet is the key to breaststroke," Gimli said, and sat down. He stared at the fire and puffed on his long dwarven pipe.

The Elvish Walk

The swimming drills that Aragorn saw in the woods of Lothlórien is the next step in learning the effective leg propulsion in breaststroke. The essence of this activity consists in using the same leg movement in all three parts (pulling up the letters "L", exposing the feelers, returning the letters "L" with the best water sensation). This activity will be a big change for the children – they do the movements they have learnt in a standing position – the letter "L", pulling up and exposing the feelers by rotating the feet and most importantly – a push from the water. The only difference is the reclining body position instead of a vertical one.

"Listen carefully! Let's see what happens when you lean forward when you float on your feelers. Do this: float on the feelers while standing, and after a while lean forward slightly. Keep moving your legs as in the standing position!"

When you lean forward, your moving legs will stay a bit behind. This will change the leg position from vertical to inclined in relation to the bottom of the pool. And now the most important thing: you will move forward using the sensation of water and the movement of the feelers which lifted you up as you switched the vertical position to a reclining one. Of course, you should maintain the structure of the leg movement that you have previously practiced in the vertical body position. In other words, if you stay afloat by moving your legs in the vertical position ("L" – the feelers – return with water sensation), and the knees did not sway to the sides, then you will be able to move forward only by changing the body position in the water while maintaining the same movement structure. There's no other way.

"So what happened after you leaned forward?"

"We started swimming forward!"

"That's right. This is how the elves swim, with their heads above the water and their legs below the water. Try swimming like this half the distance."

We do not yet use the term "breaststroke leg action". Some children may have learnt the breaststroke leg action using a different method – this may disrupt the effects of the instinctive swimming method which

involves a relatively narrow propulsive movement of the feet and excellent water sensation.

The Elvish Walk with a Spout

If the children achieve the water grip with the feet and can use it to swim forward during the elvish walk, it is time to switch them to a more hydrodynamic body position while maintaining the structure of the propulsive movement of the legs. Simply stretch the arms in front of you and place them next to the water surface. This will naturally change the position of the body – the torso and hips will be elevated a little closer to the water surface to provide better hydrodynamics and the gliding sensation at the end of the propulsive movement. The head should remain above the water all the time to effectively grip the water with the feet when extending the feelers (they won't come out of the water).

"And now make a spout with your arms. Hold your hands together so that the thumbs point to the sky, and the arms and fingers are straight. And now swim like elves, just keep your chin in the water and the spout extending in front of us."

It is likely that the children will dip the nose, eyes and forehead under the water at the end of the leg propulsion movement. There's nothing wrong with that, so do not force them to keep the whole face above the water no matter what. Just remember that, when they lift the letter "L" and extend the feelers, it is crucial that they keep the head above the water. This was what Gimli and his companion were discussing around the fire.

Head in the Speed Tunnel

The only thing left to do is to place the head under the water to ensure the best possible hydrodynamics of the glide after finishing the leg action. All previous activities were designed to teach the children to be aware when to pull up the foot (the letter "L"), rotate it (to expose the feelers) and create propulsion (a shift created by with a return movement of the feelers). This awareness will be very useful, because now the children will dip the head under the water the moment they expose the feelers, not earlier. This is crucial to learn to effectively swim the full style. How to dip the head under the water? Deep or next to the water surface, with the eyes looking down, or maybe slightly forward? You will probably shake your head in disbelief, but it does not really matter in the instinctive method. What matters is that the head stays above the water when the letters "L" are pulled up, and that it dips under the water at the end of the propulsive movement. However, do not expect the children to precisely control the head position – they should simply feel a better glide as they dip it under the water.

"Listen carefully! Who wants to try to do the same activity, but this time dip your head under the water into the speed tunnel every third shift?"

"Me, me!"

"Try this: swim like elves with a spout, but dip your head under the water every third shift. And then again do the shift with your elvish legs, with the head moving alternately over the water and under the water."

Most children will instinctively dip their head when rotating their feet and making the kicks (amore poetic term for the leg propulsion). If they do it too early, remind them to:

"Dip your head when you rotate the feelers, not earlier!"

Feeler-Tunnel

Once the children become fluent in this drill and comfortably immerse the head during the propulsive leg action, tell them to try hiding the head under the water every second kick. Once they learn how to do this drill as well, it's time for the most important activity: placing the head into the speed tunnel with each propulsive leg kick.

We have to stop for a moment and explore the intricacies of leg action coordination with the head immersion in breaststroke. The following coordination seems perfectly logical: first put your head under the water and then do the kick (it is very unfortunate that the leg propulsion is commonly called "the kick" as it is not even remotely associated with the sensation of water). However, when you look at professional breaststrokers, you can see that the moment their head enters the water coincides with the beginning of the propulsive action of rotated feet.

We will discuss this aspect of breaststroke later. As for now, one thing is certain: do not dip the head when the feet (L-letters) are pulled up towards the buttocks. Therefore, all previous fun activities were designed to make sure that the children wouldn't have any trouble setting the head position during feet rotation and in the initial phase of the propulsive movement.

"Maybe some of you will be able to dip the head into the tunnel every time the feelers rotate and make a shift? This is a kind of a feeler-tunnel. Who wants to have a try?"

In the beginning, children may experience some problems with the rhythm, because you have to take a breath before each leg propulsive movement and before submerging the head, and there is not much time for this. However, after several successful attempts, the rhythm of inhaling and then exhaling the air under water should be synchronized with the leg action.

As they raise the head to take a breath, most children will put their arms apart to "paddle" the water. It will not be a bad thing, quite the contrary – it will be the beginning of a harmonious combination of the leg action and the beginning of the

arm action.

"A glide? Did you just say what I think you said?" Gimli said, shifting his eyes from Aragorn to Legolas and back, "And where do you want to do this thing that slows you down?"

"I guess that's obvious," Aragorn replied, "When the propulsive leg action finishes, the arms and the head are streamlining, and...

"And then what?" the dwarf interrupted, "Should they be motionless until the leg propulsion dies out?"

"Well... in a way, yes..." Legolas joined in. His voice was devoid of the usual confidence.

Aragorn got up, picked up a large, heavy branch, and tossed it over the fire. Millions of sparks flew up into the starry sky.

"Gimli, you are confusing the level of training advancement and the long-distance technique," he said.

"Am I?" Gimli replied, "Or maybe you should say it more humanly?" he mocked.

Legolas smirked and looked at Aragorn.

"First of all," Aragorn said, sitting down in his usual place, "we are talking about learning the stroke, not the racing technique. And when you learn the stroke, there has to be a glide after the kick for streamlining. Secondly, there is no glide only in the 50-meter breaststroke distance; you can see the glide in a 100-meter race, and it becomes long and clear in 200-meter breaststroke racing."

"Listen to what I have to say," Gimli said, "First of all, if you teach someone breaststroke, you don't have to teach them to wait until the leg propulsion dies out. It has nothing to do with streamlining!"

Legolas was watching the dwarf closely. After a few seconds, he nodded approvingly. Seeing this, Gimli caught the wave.

"Secondly, if you ever saw a 100 meter and 200 meters breaststroke competition from under the water, you would notice an amazing phenomenon: the moment the competitors finish the leg action, they start the arm movement!"

"Maybe the dwarves do," Aragorn said a little bit, maliciously. After a moment's thought, he asked quite seriously:

"Even in a 200 meters race?"

"Even in a 200 meters race?" Gimli replied very confidently, "The first arm sweep is very calm, adjusted to the frequency of movements. The end of the leg propulsion starts the arm propulsion!" he stated.

"Aragorn, I think Gimli is right," Legolas replied calmly.

"You think so?" the dwarf shouted.

"If the end of the breaststroke leg action, however effective," Legolas continued, "won't be coordinated with the beginning of the water sensation on the palms, the propulsion continuity will be lost, as we call it in the language of the elves."

"The loss of drive continuity," Gimli repeated after Legolas, mockingly, "Elves won't say "a propulsion hole," they want to sound so sophisticated. Sports and swimming are not poetry, you hear me, elf!?"

Legolas looked at the dwarf with a smile, but said nothing. Meanwhile, Aragorn sat with his legs stretched out and looked at his shoes. He was putting soles together and then apart. When the soles came together, he imitated the movement of hands that started the sensation of water.

"It seems to me," Gimli said, looking at Aragorn, "that humans will no longer stand out from dwarves and elves in breaststroke competitions."

A thick branch that Aragorn had put to the fire broke with a loud crack. The sound resonated through the woods for a moment, then dies away. All three companions stared at the sparks, which flied again to the stars for a brief moment.

***

Dear Reader, right now you should read a sentence to let you know you are about the read the "Arm Action" section.

Unfortunately (or, in fact, "fortunately"), in the instinctive swimming method, the leg and arm action creates a complementary, harmonious whole to create a uniform forward propulsion. Therefore, you will continue with your training as if nothing has changed - well, now the arms will help a bit lift the head to take a breath and move forward.

How to take a breath more easily

"Listen carefully, now we will add something to make the breathing easier. You are going to play the game of a "feeler-tunnel", but you will help yourself with arms to raise your head for breathing."

"What? What do you mean?"

"When the head goes into the tunnel, turn your hands, make the spout, and move your arms sideways in a move that will instantly help you raise your head for a breath."

This simple message addresses the water sensation, the trajectory of the arm movement, and even the coordination of the water grip with the beginning of the head movement emerging for a breath. How is that even possible? The children will realize that the arm movement helps them raise the head, and they will instinctively look for the best water sensation to strengthen the grip. The rotated arms with thumbs down will almost make them feel it. It will also determine the best arm movement trajectory. Some will make a slightly semicircular movement, others will move the arms straight, but they will definitely feel the water. How to practice the "self-regulating" coordination of the water grip and the head lifting? A swimmer may use the arms to be able to move the head out of the water more easily. Obviously, this must be done before the head emerges from the water, not afterwards, which means coordination is not an issue. Of course, it may happen that the children make a head movement first, and only then activate the arms. They should be explained to raise the head when they start to feel thick water on the hands.

Improving the arm action

When lifting the head to breathe is naturally supported by the sensation of water on the hands (in other words, by the arm movement), proceed to the next step, which means lifting not only the head, but also the arms out of the water to take a breath. To make the matter clear, it will be difficult to teach the children to lift the shoulders high up at this stage. You should therefore focus on using the previously acquired sensation of water to lift the shoulders above the water, twisting the arms inward, without paying much attention to the specific level of the trunk above the water surface. If this is accomplished, the arms will naturally move forward in a dynamic thrust to form a spout, and the cycle will be finished.

To understand this better, let's list all components of the arm movement one by one: after the leg propulsion is completed, the arms begin to move outwards, creating the water sensation. This sensation initiates the lifting of the body for a breath, and naturally prolongs the glide. Once the outward movement of the arms finishes (the arms are in the "Y" position), and a part of the head has emerged out of the water, the arms are twisted down and inwards. All elements of the instinctive method are based on the water sensation, this "twist" will be a natural reinforcement of the water sensation and an excellent basis for raising the whole head and a part of the torso above the water level. When it's done, the final thrust of the joined arms forward is so natural that it hardly requires any practice. There is a lot of space and time to breathe – from the start of the twist to the end of the forward throw of the arms.

You may wonder why you initially teach the children to lift the head for a breath after the first outward movement of the arms, and now the head only comes out of the water as they do the twist. What is the final version? The first synchronization, called 'the breathing assistance', had a special mission to fulfil, apart from improving the sensation of water. It was designed to prevent the children from lifting the head for a breath too late, after the twist. Now that the sensation of water has increased significantly thanks to the twist, the children will naturally begin to use this moment for a full lift, instead of lifting their head when the spout starts to fall apart.

Take a moment and think about the concept in which the head is lifted for a breath as late as possible during the whole breaststroke cycle. In spite of your sincere intentions, by teaching children the so-called "delayed" breathing from the very start, you make it more difficult to synchronize the leg and arm action. As a result, the children start lifting their head to take a breath so late that they do it only when they join the arms to form a spout and thrust the arms in front of them. They then have to stop this dynamic movement to take a breath. This breaks the stroke rhythm and impairs its efficiency. When the children have mastered the art of swimming in full style, they will be able to speed up or delay the coming out of water to breathe whenever they choose to do so. Not focus on developing the sensation of water on the arms to help the children lift the head and a part of the torso above the water level without affecting the rhythm and efficiency.

A twist to lift the arms

"I have a special task for you. You will do the same "feeler-tunnel" activity you did before, and use your arms to make it easier to take a breath. Then you will not return to the spout by following the same pathway. You will do a special twist in thick water down and inwards to help you take the head and the shoulders out of the water. This is how it goes."

This demonstration is very important as you need to clearly show how the slightly bent arms move down and inwards, and finally come together to form a spout. Pay special attention to the fact that the twist is directed downwards, not backwards. This will help the children effectively lift the head and torso up above the water level and comfortably throw the arms forward.

That's a lot of new information! To be safe, repeat all parts of this activity in the correct sequence: the head is above the water, the arms held in a spout. Lift the letter "L", extend the feelers, and make a shift. While extending the sensors and making the shift, hide the head in the speed tunnel. When the head enters the speed tunnel, the legs end the propulsion movement. Then begin the outward movement of the hand to boost the water sensation and to make it easier to initiate the movement to emerge the head from the speed tunnel into the air. When the arms are in the "Y" position, twist the arms down and inwards to boost the water sensation. This will help raise the head and shoulders above the water surface. When the arms end the inward movement under the water, they naturally merge into a spout with which you dynamically move forward. You have already taken a breath, so you can put our head back to the speed tunnel, especially that as the spout has just formed.

This is the proper breaststroke cycle. Start the leg action again as you join the arms to form the spout – the next cycle will "interlock" with the former one. The end of one drill (the thrust of the spout forward along with the leg action) is also the beginning of the next one. A kind of swimming version of a Möbius strip, which ultimately develops into a full breaststroke cycle.

Chin – Forehead – Ears

The next drill is to learn how not to immerse the body too deep into the water during the glide while maintaining the best possible hydrodynamics. You will practice this skill swimming breaststroke as a full style, but with different position of the head after the breath.

"Listen carefully, you will now play a "chin – forehead – ears" game. You will swim breaststroke as a full style, but when you move your legs, you will put your head into different tunnels. First, there is a high tunnel in which only the chin goes under the water, and the eyes and forehead remain above the water. Then there is a medium tunnel in which the forehead and the eyes descend under the water. And finally, there is a deep tunnel in which you submerge the forehead, the eyes, and the ears. You will then have to look down."

To make the most of this drill, you should preferably swim two times in a row in each tunnel: chin-chin, forehead-forehead, ears-ears. This will make the body position more precise.

What is the purpose of this drill? After all, the head will slow down the leg propulsion in the chin and forehead positions. Well, this is a kind of transaction: you compromise the hydrodynamics of the glide in these body positions in exchange for high position of the shoulders and arms with the spout. In the third body position with the ears under the water and the eyes facing down the pool, the shoulders and arms will not dive very deep under the water despite the unfavorable head position as the children will remember the high movement trajectory. This will help them keep the torso slightly higher across the water, because the immersed head will lift the hips, and the arms and shoulders will be extended forward, not down.

First name and Surname – First Name – No Name

Your last task when teaching the children breaststroke within the instinctive swimming methodology is the improve the hydrodynamics of the body position in the glide. In spite of the disputes between characters from the Fellowship of the Ring, you will now allow the children to glide, to the disapproval of Gimli. The glide phase will be progressively shortened to finally obtain the best coordination of arms and legs to maintain the speed.

"When you swim the full style, your legs will at one point finish the job and come together. This is when you do the special task – when the legs and feet stick together, keep the spout glued together and look down at the bottom of the pool. Say your first name and last name in your mind and only then pull the spout apart and lift yourself up to breathe."

Again, you need to demonstrate this movement – show the children how to perform breaststroke movements with the arms and how to move the legs. When you reach the streamlined spout and head position, say your first name and surname and begin to simulate another cycle. It is important that the children say the first name and surname only after the leg propulsion has finished. This will slow down the glide, but will naturally force more streamlined body position.

Once the children have mastered this skill, shorten the time of the glide:

"Okay, and now do the same, but say your first name only instead of your first and last name!"

The slide will be cut by half, but the streamlined body position will have to be maintained. If the children feel comfortable doing this activity, the glide should be almost completely eliminated:

"Now try to swim without repeating your first name or surname."

"What? What do you mean?"

"When you finish the leg movement, start moving your arms. First the children repeated their first name and surname before starting the arm movement, then they only repeated the first name, and no they don't say anything (no name). With the end of leg action, the spout starts to disintegrate, and the arms start moving."

Some children will so concerned to shorten the glide that they start moving their arms before the leg action is finished. In this case remind the children to finish the leg movement first, and then start moving the arms.

Factum est – what happened here a moment ago

- Next to the pool:
  – placing the foot in the pull-up position to feel the water on the side of the foot and the sole;
  – rotating the foot outside for a water grip;
  – propulsive movement of the legs.
- In the water:
  – moving the legs in a vertical position;
  – developing the sensation of water on the sole and the side of the foot during downward movement;
  – optimizing the thigh and knee alignment during the leg action;
  – starting an effective propulsive movement by switching from the vertical to reclining position while keeping the water sensation and the structure of the leg action;
  – extending the body line during leg propulsion movements by stretching the arms forward to a streamlined position;
  – placing the head in a streamlined position;
  – moving the head into a streamlined position in sync with the propulsive leg action.
- Arm action:
  – activating the sensation of water by moving the arms to the outside;
  – the outward movement of the arms is synchronized with the start of head lift for breath;
  – the head and arms come out of the water by moving the arms inwards in the water;
  – thrusting the arms forward;
  – coordination of the movements of arms and legs;
  – optimizing the position of the head, shoulders and arms during the glide;
  – optimizing the glide distance and efficiency.

Epiloque

Dear Reader, you have reached the end of your journey across the unfamiliar waters of activating the swimming skills and teaching the four strokes with the instinctive swimming method. Stay here for a while. This is where your ship has brought you. Enjoy the place you're at. Every day we will discover new secrets of this world, which is dominated by the children's spontaneity and energy. The instinctive swimming method will allow you to connect with the most natural of human energies, so you and your swimmers can create this great adventure known as swimming.

Instead of an ending

I would like to list everyone who helped me create the instinctive swimming method, and this book. I would like to summarize our conversations, discussions, and arguments. I would like to tell you about coaches who are well known in the international swimming community and about those whose names no one has heard of.

I would like to tell you about working with swimmers who fought for their country at the Olympics and about young children who felt a great love for flying in the water.

I would like to tell you about young swimmers who start to believe that achieving great success in swimming is possible and about experienced athletes who, despite their age, still believe in the same thing.

I would like to tell you about masters swimmers whose passion for swimming is the purest and unsurpassed.

I would like to tell you about many people I was lucky enough to learn from.

However, instead of adding several dozen pages to this book, I will simply say this:

Ladies and gentlemen, coaches, athletes, parents, and all the wonderful people in the world of swimming who I had the privilege to meet and interact with. What I have described in this book is also the result of your work and love for the sport – Thank you!